The Little Ghost Girl

Abused Starved and Neglected.

A Little Girl Desperate for Someone to Love Her.

MAGGIE HARTLEY

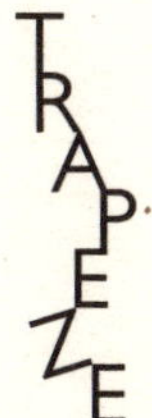

First published in Great Britain in 2016 by Orion Books,
an imprint of The Orion Publishing Group Ltd
Carmelite House, 50 Victoria Embankment,
London EC4Y 0DZ

An Hachette UK company

1 3 5 7 9 10 8 6 4 2

A CIP catalogue record for this book is
available from the British Library.

ISBN (Mass market paperback) 978 1 4091 6538 5

Typeset by Born Group

Printed and bound by CPI Group (UK) Ltd, Croydon, CR0 4YY

www.orionbooks.co.uk

Dedication

This book is dedicated to Ruth and all the children who have passed through my home. It's been a privilege to have cared for you and to be able to share your stories. And to the children who live with me now, thank you for your determination, strength and joy, and for sharing your lives with me.

Contents

A Message from Maggie

I wanted to write this book to give people an honest account of what it's like to be a foster carer. To talk about some of the challenges that I face on a day-to-day basis and some of the children like Ruth that I've helped.

I've looked after more than 200 children over the past twenty years and Ruth came to me when I'd been doing it for a decade. Her story has always stayed with me, firstly because of the horrific things that she'd been through and secondly because she was such a challenge. She pushed my little family to the limits but she also showed me that with patience, love and care, you can transform a child's life. As a foster carer, you can't change what's happened to a child in the past but you can change their future, and that's why I do it.

My main concern while writing this book was to protect the children that have been in my care. For this reason, all names and identifying details have been changed, including my own, and no locations have been included. But I can assure you that all my stories are based on real-life cases and my own experiences.

Maggie Hartley

ONE

New Arrival

It was seeing the little Babygros that got to me the most. As I pulled them out of the tumble dryer and folded them into neat piles on the bed, that's when it hit me that she'd gone.

Just over a week ago I'd said goodbye to fourteen-month-old Daniella. I'd been a foster carer for a decade now and no matter how many times I'd gone through it, it was always upsetting when a child left. Especially when it was a baby like Daniella as you couldn't help but get attached to them. She'd been with me since she was three months old and I couldn't have loved her any more if she had been my own child.

Don't get me wrong, I was delighted that she'd found a forever family and the couple who were adopting her were lovely but it didn't stop me from missing her desperately. For the past few days I'd put off sorting through her old things but now I'd finally got round to washing the piles of baby clothes, cot bedding and blankets so I could put them back into storage in the loft until the next baby came along.

Thankfully I didn't have time to dwell on my feelings as I was interrupted by a knock at the door.

'Hi, darling,' called a voice through the glass. 'Thought I'd pop round and see how you are.'

It was my friend Vicky who was also a foster carer. She lived nearby so we'd often go round to each other's houses for a cuppa and a catch-up.

'Oh, I'm fine,' I said, opening the front door and letting her in. 'I was just having a moment looking through Daniella's old things but I'm OK now.'

Vicky knew exactly what it was like when a child left. We'd both been through it so many times before and it was only natural to feel a bit low for a few days afterwards.

'How's she getting on?' she asked. 'Have you heard anything?'

'I've had a few texts and apparently she's settled in really well.'

'Ahh, bless her,' she said. 'She deserves it.'

Like most of the children who I fostered, Daniella hadn't had the best start in life. Her parents were both drug addicts and they could barely look after themselves, never mind a baby, so she'd been badly neglected for the first few months of her life. She'd come to me filthy, covered in sores from not having her nappy changed regularly, and was listless and unresponsive. By the time she left, she was a chubby, smiley little girl who'd started walking and was as bright as a button.

'I'm going to miss having a baby in the house,' I sighed.

I loved all the cuddles, the fun and the playing.

'How have Louisa and Lily taken it?' asked Vicky.

'Oh, they miss her too,' I said. 'It's really strange it being the three of us again.'

Lily was five and I'd been fostering her for the past two years. She'd been taken into care because her father was an alcoholic and violent to her mother; however, she refused to leave him. Lily looked like an angel with her big blue eyes and golden ringlets, but her behaviour had certainly been a challenge at first. She had incredible temper tantrums, threw toys and smashed things. But after living with me for a few months, she'd gradually started to calm down. She was still a lively, boisterous little thing and full of energy but she was no longer a problem.

'How's Lily getting on at school?' Vicky asked.

'Brilliantly,' I said. 'She's settled in fine and she's got a couple of little friends.'

Lily still had regular contact with her mum, and there was the hope that one day she would leave her husband and Lily could go back and live with her, but that hadn't happened yet. I'd realised early on that her issue was all about attention. Her mum suffered from depression and I think Lily's behaviour was an attempt to get her to notice her. Now she was a happy, settled five-year-old and I didn't want to disrupt that and have her go back to square one, which was likely to happen if she went to live with her mum again.

My other placement was fourteen-year-old Louisa who had come to me around the same time as Lily. Sadly her parents had both died in a car crash. Alone and struggling to cope with her grief, she was painfully shy at first but she had started to enjoy school and had a nice group of mates.

Our little family rubbed along nicely. Louisa treated Lily like a sister and was very protective of her and Lily adored her. Also, because they were different ages, they needed me in different ways, which made for a good balance. However, I knew it wouldn't be long before things changed again.

'Now Daniella's gone I expect I'll be offered another placement any minute,' I told Vicky.

'Yep,' she said. 'You should enjoy the peace and quiet while it lasts.'

I was a single foster carer so I had to cope with challenging children on my own. But I loved every minute of it and, without sounding like too much of a big head, I was damn good at my job. Social Services would often give me the children that nobody else could handle. I was always busy and my four-bedroom terrace was never empty, but that's the way I liked it.

Getting a new child was exciting but I was also a tiny bit apprehensive at the same time. Whenever a new placement arrived, the dynamic of the house changed and it always took a few weeks for everyone to settle and find their place in the new pecking order.

'Right, I must go,' said Vicky, drinking up the last dregs of her tea. 'Before you know it, it'll be three twenty and the kids will have finished school.'

'I must get on too,' I said. 'I need to get this baby stuff packed away.'

'Good luck,' said Vicky.

After she'd gone I cracked on with my sorting. I was about to tackle the toy box when the phone rang.

'Maggie, it's Mike Mitchell. How are you?'

'Fine, thanks,' I said.

Mike was the fostering manager at the local authority. I'd worked with him for years and we knew each other well.

'What can I do for you?' I asked, although I suspected that I already knew the answer to that one.

'I've got a bit of a sensitive case that I thought you might be able to help with.'

'Go on,' I said. 'I'm all ears.'

I listened as he explained they were looking for a placement for an eleven-year-old girl who had just been taken into care.

'This morning she made some serious allegations to her teacher and she's currently being questioned at the police station,' he said.

'What's she alleging took place?' I asked.

'To be honest, Maggie, that's all I know at the minute,' he said. 'The allegations are serious enough to mean that she can't go home so we need to find somewhere to place her. By all accounts, she's a bit of a tricky character and she'll need to be handled sensitively.'

He paused.

'So,' he said. 'What do you think?'

'I'll take her,' I said without any hesitation. 'You know me, Mike, I like a challenge.'

'Great,' he said. 'I thought you'd say that so she's already on her way to your house with a police officer and her social worker.'

'Well, it's a bloomin' good job I said yes then, isn't it?' I laughed. 'What time do you think they'll be here?'

I was already running through a mental checklist of all the things I liked to do before a new placement arrived.

'I reckon they'll be with you in the next ten minutes,' he said.

'Ten minutes?' I gasped. 'I'd better hang up and get cracking then.'

Good God, I thought to myself, *talk about giving me time to prepare.*

'Oh and, Mike,' I said, 'what's her name?'

'I'm sorry, Maggie, I don't even know that much,' he told me apologetically.

It was frustrating but I'd learnt by now that was the nature of the job. When a child was taken into care very suddenly sometimes you didn't know anything about them before they turned up on your doorstep.

'There is one other issue that I should quickly mention,' he said. 'Her family only live ten minutes away from you. Do you think that will be a problem?'

'I shouldn't think so,' I told him. 'It's a different neighbourhood so they'll probably use different shops and supermarkets to us. Now let me go so I can at least attempt to get things sorted.'

I put the phone down and tried not to panic. I hoped ten minutes was a slight exaggeration and that it might be an hour before they arrived. I rushed upstairs to give the spare room the once-over but thankfully it was all spick and span. After Daniella had left I'd given it a good tidy. I'd taken the cot down, and the bunk and single bed had clean bedding on them. The woodchip walls were painted magnolia so were a blank canvas. I tended to personalise a room once a child had been with me for a few weeks and I knew a bit more about them and their likes and dislikes.

As I smoothed down the duvets and plumped up the pillows, I wondered what sort of state this poor girl was going to be in. She'd gone off to school this morning as normal and now her whole world had changed. She wasn't allowed to go back home or see her family and had been subjected to hours of questioning by the police. God only knows what sort of allegations she'd made and against whom. Whatever they were, I suspected she was going to be very fragile and traumatised.

I went to the cupboard where I kept all my supplies and grabbed a new toothbrush, some towels and a flannel. I was laying them out on the bed when I heard a knock at the door.

I looked at my watch. Mike hadn't been joking when he'd said ten minutes. I gave the room a quick, last-minute check, opened the window to let in some fresh air and then dashed downstairs.

I opened the front door to find a female police officer in uniform and another woman standing there. Between them was a small, unkempt little girl.

'Hello, I'm Liz Fleming, the social worker,' she said, showing me her ID.

'This is PC Clare Smith and this . . .' she said, pointing to the girl, '. . . is Ruth.'

She was a tiny little thing, stick thin with elfin features and a pale face. Mike had already told me that she was eleven but if he hadn't I would have said she was at least three or four years younger. She stared up at me with weary blue eyes. Her black hair was long and straggly and she was wearing school uniform that had seen better days. There was a ring of dirt around the neck of her grubby white shirt, her nylon skirt was all crumpled and her shoes were falling apart.

'Hello, Ruth,' I said. 'Come on in.'

I ushered them all into the hallway.

'This is Maggie,' Liz told Ruth. 'You're going to be staying with her for a while.'

'Cool.' She shrugged.

The door to the living room was open and, to my surprise, she wandered in and had a good look around.

'Ooh, this place is swish,' she said. 'I like your telly.'

'Oh, er, thanks,' I said, slightly taken aback by her confidence. She might have looked like she wouldn't say boo to a goose but she seemed bold and sure of herself – not what I had been expecting at all.

'Come into the kitchen and I'll get you all a drink,' I said.

Ruth sauntered through and proceeded to pick up all my ornaments on the dresser and examine them. She even read a couple of thank you cards that people had sent me.

'So, where's my room gonna be then?' she asked. 'You see, I ain't got any of my clothes with me. I haven't even got no pyjamas or nuffink.'

'Don't worry,' I told her. 'We'll sort something out.'

'I'm sure Maggie will grab some bits for you at the shops tomorrow,' said Liz.

'Great,' said Ruth. 'I'd love some new clothes.'

Watching her swaggering around my kitchen, you'd never have guessed what she'd been through that day. She certainly wasn't the traumatised young girl that I'd been expecting. She seemed to be taking it all in her stride and was treating going into care like one big adventure.

'Who would like a cuppa?' I asked, flicking the kettle on. 'Ruth, would you like a drink? I've got some water or juice.'

'No, ta,' she said. 'What's for dinner then? When are we having that?'

'Oh, I haven't thought about it yet,' I said. 'I'll probably do some pasta a little bit later on.'

Just then I heard a key in the front door. It was Louisa coming back from school. Lily was at a friend's house for a play date.

'We're in the kitchen, lovey,' I shouted.

She looked surprised when she saw the group of people standing there.

'Louisa, this is Ruth,' I said. 'She's going to be staying with us for a while.'

'Hi,' said Louisa. She spoke shyly but she wasn't fazed at all. She'd been living with me long enough to be used to kids coming and going, and she knew not to ask any questions.

'Perhaps you can take Ruth into the front room and see what's on telly?' I suggested.

It would give me a chance to chat to Liz and PC Smith in private to see if they could tell me any more than Mike had been able to.

'Cool,' said Ruth, following her without a second glance.

I turned to the two women.

'Tea?' I said.

'I won't stay as I've got to get back to the station,' said PC Smith. 'But these are the dates and times that we'll need to pick Ruth up and take her for questioning.'

She handed me a long list that seemed to take up most of the coming week.

'What about school?' I asked.

'She'll be off this week while she gives her statement then after that we'll see,' said Liz. 'I think it's unlikely that she'll be going back to the same school as that's where her siblings go.'

'I'll be back to collect her in the morning,' said PC Smith before she left.

As I saw her out, I glanced in the living room to check on the girls. The telly was on and Ruth was chatting away to Louisa.

'She's a talkative little thing,' I said to Liz.

'She certainly is,' she said. 'I only met her this afternoon so I still don't have the full picture of what's been going on at home.'

'What do you know so far?' I asked.

Liz explained that Ruth had lived with her stepmother Marie, her dad Ian and four other siblings.

'Three of them were her stepmum's biological children and then there was Ruth and her older brother David,' she said.

'How come she was living with her dad?' I asked. 'Where's her mum?'

'Well,' said Liz. 'That's where it gets more complicated.

'From what little I know so far, Ruth's mother Sharon left when Ruth was six, when she found out her husband was cheating on her with her friend Marie.

'When Mum left, Ian moved in with Marie and she took on his two children – Ruth and David. Then they went on to have three more children of their own: three boys.'

Liz explained that the case had come to light after Ruth's teachers had called the police and Social Services earlier that day after she'd told them something at school.

'What was the nature of the allegations she was making?' I asked.

'Now that, I'm afraid, I don't know,' she said. 'Whatever it was, it was serious enough to warrant Ruth being removed immediately from her family and taken into care.

'I picked her up from the police station and brought her here but a colleague has promised to give me a proper debrief in the morning so I'll update you then.

'I do know that it's been a long, hard day for Ruth so she probably just wants to sleep.'

'She seems to have handled it OK,' I said.

'Yes,' said Liz. 'She's clearly a resilient little thing.'

I walked Liz through to the front room where she said goodbye to the girls.

'I'll see you tomorrow, Ruth, when I come and take you to the police station.'

'Yeah great,' said Ruth.

We went out into the hallway.

'Any problems, then give me a ring, Maggie,' she told me. 'I'll find out as much as I can tomorrow and fill you in.

'But, as you know, as there's an ongoing police investigation, you can't talk to Ruth about the allegations she's made or ask her any questions about them.'

I nodded. That was standard procedure just in case there was a court case eventually and Ruth was called to give evidence.

'But if she brings anything up of her own accord you can listen and make a note of it.'

'No problem,' I said. 'I'll talk to you tomorrow.'

After I'd seen her out I went to check on the girls again.

'How are we all doing in here?' I asked.

'Alright,' said Ruth. 'Do you know when dinner's gonna be, cos I'm starving?'

'I'll go and put some pasta on now,' I said. 'Then we've got to pick up Lily.'

'Who's she?' asked Ruth.

'She's a little five-year-old that I look after,' I explained to her. 'She lives here with Louisa and me.'

'I've got a big brother, who's fifteen,' she said. 'And I've got three little brothers.'

She frowned.

'The police said my big brother's been taken into care too. Do you know where he is, Maggie?'

Liz had mentioned Ruth's brother David but I didn't realise that he'd been removed from the family home too.

'I'm so sorry, I don't have any idea,' I said. 'But how about I make some calls in the morning and see if I can find out?'

Ruth nodded.

'Right,' I said. 'I'd better get this pasta on.'

As I boiled some pasta and heated up some sauce in a pan, I thought about Ruth and how seemingly unfazed she was about what she'd been through. She was treating being taken into care and questioned by the police as if it were a normal, everyday occurrence. It just didn't add up.

'Dinner's ready,' I called when everything was on the table.

Both girls ate up. Ruth was very thin and I wondered whether food had been in short supply at home.

'When you've finished, please put your plates on the side,' I said.

Ruth brought her plate over to the side, but then dropped it into the stainless steel sink, where it broke into two pieces.

'Oh well,' she said casually, wandering off. 'You can get another one.'

I was shocked at how blasé she was about it. Most kids when they are in a new place tiptoe around for their first few days and would be mortified if they broke anything, but Ruth walked around like she owned the place. I know accidents happen but what disturbed me was her attitude. She didn't even say sorry. Her view was that I could just replace it. It made me uneasy.

After I'd washed up, we all got in the car and went to pick up Lily from her friend's house.

'Lily, this is Ruth,' I told her. 'She's going to come and live with us for a while.'

Like Louisa, she just accepted that and gave her a big smile.

When we got home, I got Lily bathed and put her into bed while the older girls watched telly. We all watched *Coronation Street* together and at around 8.30 p.m. I decided it was time for Ruth to get ready for bed.

'There's clean towels on the bed and a flannel and a toothbrush,' I told her. 'You go and get washed and then let's get you to bed.'

'Already?' she moaned.

'You've had a long day,' I said gently. 'And you've got to go back to the police station again tomorrow for more questioning.'

'Yeah.' She grinned. 'That lady Liz said I get to have the whole week off school.'

I took her upstairs and handed her some clean pyjamas that I'd borrowed from Louisa. She went off into the bathroom. When she came out in them she looked so skinny and frail. They were hanging of her bony frame and I could see some small purple bruises on her arms and around her neck.

What had this poor girl been through? I thought as she wandered into her bedroom.

Someone had clearly hurt her and I was keen to find out who.

'Would you like me to tuck you in or kiss you goodnight?' I asked, poking my head around the door.

'No thanks,' she said bluntly.

'Night night then,' I said.

She didn't say anything and turned over to face the wall.

I left her door ajar and the landing light on and went downstairs.

What I'd seen of Ruth so far had intrigued me. Often when children are taken into care suddenly they are very fearful but she didn't seem to be.

However, one thing I was sure of was that this confident attitude and swaggering around was just a façade. It was a front that Ruth had put on to protect herself from what was happening. I'd no doubt she was scared and vulnerable after everything she'd been put through, but for some reason she couldn't show it.

On the outside she didn't seem shaken or upset – in fact her behaviour since she'd arrived had been quite brattish. She wasn't acting like a traumatised child, but I knew from past experience that the way kids acted when they were first placed with me wasn't always a true reflection of how they were.

I needed to find out more about what she'd been through and why she'd been taken into care so quickly. Then maybe I'd know what I was dealing with here. Because, at this point in time, I didn't have a clue.

TWO

Questions and Confusion

A new person in the house always meant a restless night's sleep for me. It wasn't as if Ruth was a toddler or a baby but it took me a while to get used to someone else's noises and at first I always had one ear listening out in case of any problems. I was very conscious of how Ruth must be feeling too. Despite all her bravado, she was in a strange house with strange people after having had a traumatic day so I wanted her to feel as settled as possible given the situation.

However, she seemed fine. I checked on her before I went to bed and she was fast asleep. I didn't hear a peep from her but I had a disturbed night, tossing and turning, thinking things over in my head. I didn't know what to make of this girl. She gave the impression of being frail but at the same time she was so cocky and full of attitude. It didn't add up and I was curious about what was to come. What I *was* sure about was that I wasn't getting the full picture and there was a lot more to Ruth than met the eye.

The next morning I got up as normal with Lily and Louisa but there wasn't a sound from Ruth's room.

'Where's that big girl?' Lily asked.

'You mean Ruth?' I said. 'She's still in bed. She had a hard day yesterday so I'm letting her have a bit of a lie-in.'

The police weren't coming to collect her until later on so I decided to let her sleep. I made breakfast for the other two and helped Lily get dressed in her uniform. Thankfully one of her friends' mums had offered to take her to school for me when she'd heard we'd got a new child arriving.

Just after nine, when everyone else had gone, I gently tapped on Ruth's door.

'Are you OK in there?' I called. 'Time to get up now.'

Eventually she staggered out onto the landing looking bleary-eyed.

'Where are the others?' she asked.

'They've gone to school,' I said. 'How are you today?'

She shrugged her shoulders and scowled at me.

I handed her her school uniform that I'd washed, dried and ironed so it looked a bit more presentable. I knew Louisa's clothes would be way too big for her so it was all she had for now.

'I know you're not going to school today but you'll have to put this on for the time being,' I said.

'Ain't you got any other clothes?' she sighed. 'The social worker said you were gonna get me some new stuff.'

'I'm afraid I haven't had the chance yet,' I told her. 'When you're at the police station later I'll go out and get you a few bits and then at the weekend I'll take you shopping so you can choose some clothes yourself.'

'Yeah, alright,' she said. 'Can you make me some breakfast now?'

The way she spoke to me was very dismissive but I knew I had to be tolerant. She was a frightened, damaged eleven-year-old whose world had just been turned upside down so I had to be patient.

'Of course I'll get you some breakfast but let me show you where everything is first,' I told her.

I took her into the bathroom and showed her how the shower worked and where the shampoo and the shower gel were.

'In this house we like people to have a shower or a bath every day to keep themselves clean,' I said.

Then I showed her the laundry basket where we put our dirty clothes at the end of the day.

'Everyone mucks in,' I told her. 'So it would be great if you could make your bed in the morning and sometimes I might ask you to put your clean washing away in your drawers.'

I found giving children little jobs like that to do gave them a sense of ownership and responsibility for their things.

Ruth rolled her eyes but I hoped that she'd taken it all in.

'What time are the police coming for me today?' she asked.

'Not until eleven,' I said. 'So you've got plenty of time. Now you go and get yourself a shower while I make you some breakfast.'

I went back downstairs and poured a glass of orange juice and got out some bread to toast for her. Five minutes later Ruth appeared, fully dressed.

'Wow that was speedy,' I said.

'Yeah, I just had a quick shower,' she told me.

But her hair wasn't wet at all, not even a bit damp at the ends, and I suspected that she'd been nowhere near the shower.

'Did you manage to work it OK?' I asked.

'Hmm,' she mumbled.

While she was eating her breakfast, I nipped upstairs to the loo and I couldn't help but give her flannel and towel a quick feel. They were both bone dry and the shower didn't have a drop of water in it. Ruth clearly hadn't washed herself but I knew it was way too soon to pull her up on it. She'd just got here and she was facing hours of police questioning today, which I knew was going to be hard for her. It wasn't going to kill her to skip a shower for one day so I decided to keep quiet for now.

'Did you sleep OK?' I asked her as I made her a cheese sandwich for her packed lunch.

'Yeah,' she said. 'It was nice havin' a bed.'

'What do you mean?' I asked, puzzled. 'Didn't you have a bed at home?'

'My brothers did but I wasn't allowed to,' she said. 'They had bunk beds but I had to sleep downstairs in the living room.'

Surely that couldn't be right . . .

'So you were on a mattress?' I asked.

She shook her head.

'I had to wait while everyone else was in bed then I slept on the settee. It was a bit lumpy and I was always rolling off but if I moaned I got a good hiding.'

'Well, that doesn't sound very comfy at all,' I said.

I couldn't believe what I was hearing and I knew this was something I needed to mention to Liz. I made a mental note to give her a call as soon as Ruth had been collected.

'The police will be here soon so you need to go and brush your teeth,' I told her when she'd finished her breakfast.

But instead of going and doing as I asked, Ruth sat there.

'Did you hear me, lovey?' I asked. 'Please go and do your teeth.'

Ruth sighed and got up but instead of heading upstairs, she stood in front of me with her arms folded and a defiant look on her face. She didn't say anything but I could see that she was challenging me. I wasn't prepared to get involved in a stand-off so I busied myself clearing the breakfast plates away and eventually she got the message and went upstairs.

Five minutes later PC Smith arrived to collect Ruth.

'How's she been?' she asked.

'OK,' I said. 'She seems to be making herself at home.'

'Ruth,' I called up the stairs. 'PC Smith's here to take you to the police station.'

Eventually she came down.

'Here's your packed lunch' I said, handing her the lunch box. 'Did you remember to brush your teeth?'

'Yep,' she said unconvincingly, looking down at the floor.

It was another thing that I needed keep an eye on to add to my list.

'We're going to meet Liz down at the station,' PC Smith told me. 'I should have Ruth back here by three at the latest.'

'No problem. I hope it goes OK, Ruth,' I told her and she gave me a weak smile.

I watched them as they walked down the street towards the car.

'Will Liz take me for a McDonald's?' I heard Ruth ask. 'She promised she'd take me for a Maccy D's if I answered all your questions today.'

'Well, I'm not sure about that,' I heard PC Smith say as I shut the door.

I didn't envy PC Smith. I felt for Ruth, I really did. I didn't even know the full extent of what she'd been through yet but she didn't exactly endear herself to people.

I gave Liz a ring, hoping that I'd catch her before Ruth arrived.

'Maggie, I'm so sorry I haven't had chance to call you yet,' she said. 'I've just had a quick debrief with another social worker and the police about Ruth and I've finally got some information to share with you.'

'Great,' I said. 'There are also a couple of things I wanted to mention to you.'

'I've got to go in a minute to sit in on Ruth's interviews so can I possibly pop round later for a chat? Is lunchtime any good?'

'That's fine,' I said. Ruth would still be at the police station then so we would be able to talk in private.

In the meantime, I went into town as I needed to get her some clothes to tide her over the next few days. I whizzed around the shops and picked her up some socks and pants, some pyjamas and a dressing gown, a couple of tops, some jeans and a skirt. I'd just walked through the door at one o'clock when Liz pulled up outside.

'How's it going?' I asked, putting down my carrier bags. 'How's Ruth been this morning?'

'It's horrendous for her but the police are being very patient,' she said.

'So tell me,' I said. 'Do you know any more about why she was taken into care?'

Liz and I sat down at the kitchen table and she told me the whole story. All my years of fostering meant that I'd dealt with some traumatic cases but it never failed to upset me when I heard some of the horrendous things children had been put through by the adults who were supposed to be the ones who loved and cared for them.

'Ruth was at school yesterday when a teacher noticed some bloodstains on her skirt,' she said. 'Assuming that she'd started her periods, she sent her to see the school nurse but Ruth was adamant that although she had recently started her periods, that wasn't what it was.

'She told them very matter-of-factly that she was bleeding because of what her dad had done to her.

'She said it often happened when he'd been "loving her too much",' said Liz sadly.

I shuddered at the language she'd used. *Poor, poor kid*. From the way Ruth had described it, it was clear to me that the abuse must have been going on for quite a while.

'Her school called the police and they questioned her and a medical examination confirmed that she had internal injuries consistent with being sexually abused.

'Both old and new injuries.'

Ruth's father Ian was denying the allegations. He'd been arrested yesterday afternoon and Social Services had immediately taken her into care.

'One thing I wanted to mention was when she came out of the bathroom last night I noticed that she had bruises around her neck,' I said.

'Sadly it looks like Dad was also violent to her,' said Liz. 'As well as sexually abusing her, he gave her one heck of a beating.'

'That poor girl,' I sighed. 'What does her stepmum say about all of this?'

'She's sticking by her husband and says Ruth is a fantasist, that she's always been trouble and is making it all up.'

Poor child. Not only had she been through that, but the woman she thought of as her mum didn't even believe her.

'The police want to get Ruth's statement as quickly as possible while everything is still fresh in her mind,' said Liz. 'The good news is, even at this early stage it looks like there's enough evidence for Dad to be charged.'

I wasn't sure if that was good news or not. If he kept denying it, that meant there would eventually be a trial. More trauma for Ruth to cope with.

'I'm so sorry, Maggie, but I have to get back to the station now to sit in on the police interviews with Ruth, but do keep in touch,' said Liz.

'No problem,' I said.

'Oh, Liz, there's just one more thing,' I added. 'Ruth mentioned that her older brother David has been taken into care too and she was asking about where he is.'

'He's with another foster carer,' she said. 'We thought it was best to remove both of Dad's children from the home until we find out more.

'Unfortunately, until Ruth's finished giving her statement the police don't want her and David to meet up, in case they compare notes.

'When the police have finished their questioning we'll definitely arrange for them to see each other.'

She explained that David had already given his statement to the police.

'It seems that he was subject to violence at the hands of his father but not sexual abuse,' Liz told me. 'He doesn't seem to be aware that Ruth had been abused by their dad.'

'What about Ruth's half-brothers?' I asked.

'There's no suggestion or evidence that Dad touched the others. From what we've seen they all appear to be happy, healthy and well cared for. So, for now, while Dad's in custody we've said they can remain in the family home with Mum.'

The plot thickened and by the time Liz had left, my head was spinning. Ruth had clearly been through a horrendous time at the hands of her own father. Why hadn't she been happy, healthy and well cared for like her half-siblings?

I was starting to understand that her bolshy attitude was a defence mechanism but it wasn't making her any friends. When Ruth got home from the police station that afternoon I was making her a drink and a snack in the kitchen when Louisa came in.

'Ruth is doing my head in.'

'Just be as patient as you can with her,' I said. 'She's been through a lot and this is all very new to her.'

'Alright, I'll try,' she sighed. 'She's just so cocky and she never stops talking and it's all really confusing.'

'What do you mean?' I asked.

'Well, you said she lived with her stepmum but she keeps talking about her mum,' she said. 'And when I mentioned her stepmum she got really narky with me.'

'I've been told she lived with her dad and his wife,' I said. 'Maybe she still sees her biological mum from time to time?'

I was beginning to question the facts myself so I decided to ask her and clear it up. I went back into the living room with Louisa.

'Ruth, lovey,' I said, 'before you came here, you lived with your dad and your stepmother, didn't you?'

Her face crumpled up in anger.

'I wish people would stop saying that,' she sighed. 'The police have been saying it all day. I don't understand why everyone's calling her my stepmum. She's my *mum*.'

Alarm bells started ringing inside my head. I told myself I needed to be completely certain about this before I rang Liz.

'Let me double-check Ruth. What do you call Marie – the lady who lived with you in the same house as you and your dad? She's your stepmother, isn't she?'

'I don't know what you mean,' Ruth shouted, getting angrier by the minute. 'Why are you saying she's my stepmother? She's my mum.'

I knew then we had a major problem. I went into the kitchen and rang Liz straight away.

'There's something I need to check with you,' I told her. 'Does Ruth definitely know that Marie is her stepmother and not her mum? She seems very confused.'

'Well, she was six when her mum left and they moved in there so I assumed that she did,' said Liz. 'We've always referred to Marie as her stepmum and so have the police during questioning.'

'Liz, I honestly don't think she knows,' I said. 'As far as she's concerned, that woman is her mum and she's getting cross with anyone who says otherwise. I think you need to come and have a chat with her.'

'I will do,' said Liz. 'I'll drop in on my way home.'

Poor Ruth. She'd already been through so much in the past couple of days. God only knows what effect a bombshell like this was going to have on her.

The doorbell rang half an hour later.

'That will probably be Liz,' I told Ruth. 'She wanted to come round and see you.'

'Again?' she sighed.

I let Liz in and the three of us sat in the front room.

'Hi, Ruth,' said Liz. 'I wanted to quickly talk to you about your stepmother.'

Ruth rolled her eyes.

'I've told you all,' she said through gritted teeth 'I don't have a stepmum.'

'Who was the lady that lived with you and your brother and your dad?' I asked.

'That's my mum, Marie,' she said.

Liz and I looked at each other.

'Ruth, can you remember when you were little? When you were six, you, your dad and David moved in with your mum's friend Marie,' said Liz.

Ruth didn't say a word, she just looked confused.

'Marie took on the role of your mum when she married your dad but she's not your real mother, is she?

'Your real mum Sharon left when you were little.'

Ruth started to look furious.

'That's not true,' she snapped.

'It is, Ruth,' said Liz gently. 'We don't know where your real mum Sharon is but it's her friend Marie who is now married to your dad and has been bringing you and your brother up for all these years.'

Ruth looked shocked and angry.

'No!' she shouted. 'I've told you. The lady who I lived with is my mum. You're lying.'

No matter what Liz said or how gently she tried to explain it, Ruth was having none of it. In the end she got so upset, she stormed out of the room.

'I'm sorry about that, Maggie,' said Liz. 'We honestly thought she knew. David definitely does and we assumed that she was old enough to remember. We didn't realise that it wasn't something that was openly discussed at home.'

'Maybe she does know but she's in denial,' I said. 'Sometimes things are too painful for children to deal with so they refuse to accept them.'

Even after Liz had told her that Marie was not her mum, Ruth refused point-blank to accept it. And if I tried to suggest otherwise she got very angry.

'You mean my mum,' she'd correct me. 'That stupid social worker's a liar.'

The only thing that I was sure of in all this was that Ruth was one confused little girl. Perhaps this was her way of dealing with the traumatic home life that she'd had. Her coping mechanism was to believe her version of events so she didn't have to face reality. It certainly made it extremely confusing for the rest of us. I was also sure it was only the tip of the iceberg and there was a lot more we had yet to discover about what had gone on at Ruth's house.

THREE

Hidden Horrors

The doorbell rang and I looked at my watch. It was 3 p.m. on the dot so I knew exactly who it would be.

'Hello, lovey,' I said opening the door to Ruth. 'How did it go today?'

She gave me a weak smile. I knew the police were being as gentle as possible with her but five days into being interviewed, I could see that she was absolutely exhausted.

'You look tired,' I told her. 'Why don't you go up to your room for a lie-down?'

She stared up at me with her big, hollow, blue eyes and nodded. As I looked back at her, it was almost as if I could see straight through her. She was a little ghost of a girl. Her eyes were blank and devoid of any emotion, as if she'd withdrawn from life and the world, and her skin was so pale it was almost translucent.

Ruth was obviously weary because, for once, she didn't argue with me and she disappeared off upstairs to her bedroom.

'How's it going?' I asked Liz, who'd driven her back.

'Very slowly,' she sighed. 'I know it must be awful for her but some days she refuses to co-operate or answer any questions which is why it's dragging on for so long. The police are being very patient.'

'It must be so hard for her having to relive everything,' I said.

I knew they would have been handling her as sensitively as possible but the fact was, if they wanted to secure a conviction against her father, they needed every little detail of the physical and sexual abuse she had suffered for God knows how long.

Ruth was a confused, angry girl but she was still only eleven years old. I could only imagine how traumatic and upsetting it must have been for her to go over events time and time again.

'And you're being careful, aren't you, not to discuss anything about the abuse?' asked Liz.

I nodded.

'It's tricky as I want her to trust me and feel like she can open up, but when she comes home I don't ask her anything,' I told her. 'I've tried to explain to Ruth that it's not because I don't care but because I'm not allowed to, but I'm not sure that she gets it.

'To be honest, she hasn't volunteered much. As you can see, she's shattered when she comes home so I'm trying to keep everything as quiet as possible for her.'

'As and when I know more I'll obviously update you,' said Liz. 'The police are getting to the point where they think they've got enough, so hopefully Ruth will have finished giving her statement by early next week.'

'Good,' I said. 'Also, there was something else that I wanted to mention to you but I didn't have the chance the other day.'

I explained what Ruth had said about not having her own bed at home and having to sleep on the sofa in the living room.

'It's funny you should say that,' said Liz. 'I've just had a debrief with the police and they're now looking at the possibility of pursuing charges of neglect against her stepmother Marie.

'Ruth talked about the sleeping arrangements when she was being interviewed and there were some other things she mentioned that suggested she wasn't treated very well at home.'

'What sort of things?' I asked.

'It seems Marie resented those two kids from the day they moved in and, as the years have gone by, her treatment of Ruth in particular has got worse.

'She told the police that when everyone else went out, she wasn't allowed to go with them and had to stay at home and do chores. Things like the washing-up and the hoovering.

'She spent most of her time in her bedroom and if she didn't do as she was told, she was beaten by her father.'

I couldn't believe what I was hearing.

'It sounds like Cinderella and her wicked stepmother,' I sighed.

'Yes, I suppose it is a bit,' said Liz. 'By all accounts, the three biological children were all treated well and even Ruth's brother David was looked after OK.

'She had a medical when she was taken into care that showed she was underweight and small for her age. From what we can gather, Ruth got fed – in that she got enough to stop her from starving. However, she was often denied meals as a punishment.

'From what she's telling us, she didn't get any of the warmth, the treats and the love that her half-brothers did.'

'Poor kid,' I sighed.

It was no wonder Ruth felt angry at the world.

'Also, Maggie, before I go there's something else I wanted to talk to you about,' said Liz.

She paused.

'How can I put this? It's a bit of a delicate matter.'

I knew straight away what she was going to say.

'Is it the personal hygiene issue?' I asked, and Liz nodded.

'I didn't want to mention it but I think it's getting to the point where someone needs to say something to Ruth,' she said.

'Don't worry. It's on my radar,' I told her. 'I was giving her the first few days to settle in but now I know I need to take more drastic action.'

'Thanks, Maggie,' she said. 'It's a tricky one.'

The fact was, Ruth was starting to smell. Every day I had asked her if she'd had a shower and brushed her teeth and she'd nod or mutter yes but I knew that she hadn't. She did her best to convince me, though. In the evening, she'd leave her dirty clothes in a heap on the bathroom floor, in order to give the impression that she'd had a shower even though the shower and her towel weren't wet. I washed her clothes so I knew the smell wasn't because she was wearing dirty things. However, by now you couldn't fail to notice it. Before Ruth walked into a room, you could smell her before you saw her, and the smell would linger long after she'd gone. I'd send her off to the police station on a morning in clean clothes that smelt of washing powder but by the time she came home in the afternoon, the stench was back. It'd got so strong now that even clean clothes couldn't mask it. I'd been trying the softly softly approach but even the other kids had started to notice. Louisa had commented on it and Lily refused to sit next to her on the sofa any more. It was time to take decisive action.

After Liz had gone I went upstairs to check on Ruth. As I peeped around her bedroom door, the smell hit me again. The whole room reeked.

Ruth lay fast asleep on the bed. For all her bravado and cockiness, when I looked at her like this, a tiny little slip of a thing curled up on her bed, I knew it was all a front. I was sure there was more to her lack of personal hygiene than first met the eye. She was an eleven-year-old who had been abused, beaten and neglected. I knew her hygiene problems were all linked to that and her low self-esteem. How, though, could I tackle her problems and get to the root of them without talking about the abuse and what had happened to her? It was an impossible situation.

Ruth was in such a deep sleep that I had to wake her at 5.30 p.m. for dinner. Groggily she came downstairs and plonked herself at the table next to Lily.

'Yuck, you smell of poo,' she said, wrinkling her nose in disgust.

'No I don't,' she said.

'Lily, that's not very kind,' I told her.

'But it's true,' she said.

The sad fact was Lily had hit the nail on the head. Ruth did smell of poo, mixed in with the stench of body odour and general dirt. I knew she couldn't carry on like this.

That evening, before Ruth's bedtime, I went up to the bathroom, got her toothbrush and squeezed some toothpaste on it.

'Ruth, can you come up and do your teeth, please?' I called.

She frowned when she saw her toothbrush laid out by the sink with the toothpaste already on it.

'Now, you've been telling me that you've been brushing your teeth but I honestly don't think you have,' I said.

'Yeah I have,' she snapped.

'Well, how come every day when I've checked your toothbrush it's been dry?' I said. 'I've decided that if I can't trust you to do them then I'll have to do them myself.'

I picked up the brush from the side.

'Open wide, please,' I said.

Ruth scowled at me.

'You're not brushing my teeth like a baby,' she told me. 'Give it here and I'll do it.'

'OK,' I said, handing it to her. 'But I'm going to stay here and make sure that you're giving them a proper brush.'

Begrudgingly she lifted the toothbrush to her mouth and slowly started brushing her teeth.

'I'm going to get some clean towels out of the airing cupboard but I'll still be listening,' I told her.

As I walked out onto the landing, I heard Ruth kick the side of the bath.

'Are you OK in there?' I shouted.

'Fine,' she mumbled through a mouthful of toothpaste.

However, I could tell that she was fuming. She was cross with me for realising what she was doing and angry at the fact that she couldn't get out of it any more. Well, she certainly wasn't going to like what was about to happen next.

After she'd finished brushing her teeth, I turned the shower on and handed her a towel.

'Put this towel around you, hand me your dirty clothes and then get in the shower, please,' I said.

'No,' she said. 'I don't want to. You'll have to make me.'

I knew I couldn't physically force her to have a shower so I needed a different approach. All I could do was be honest with her and tell her the truth, no matter how brutal.

'Ruth, you need to have a shower because you smell,' I said. 'It's got to the point where other people have started to notice and it's not fair on you or us. It's not hygienic.'

I wasn't doing it to be cruel. It was crueller to leave her like that and have other people make hurtful comments.

'I don't smell,' she yelled.

'Ruth, I'm afraid you do, so you need to have a good wash with some soap and a flannel and then shampoo your hair so you're nice and clean,' I said.

'Now I'm going to leave the bathroom so you can get undressed but I'm going to come back in a couple of minutes and check that you get in that shower.'

I walked out onto the landing.

'Ready?' I called after a while but she didn't say anything.

When I went back in, Ruth was standing there with the towel around her. She threw her clothes at me.

'Now get in the shower, please,' I said, turning my head away and holding open the door for her.

She stepped in and slammed the cubicle door and I left her to it. A few minutes later the bathroom door flew open and Ruth stomped across the landing to her bedroom. She could only have been in there for a few minutes but her hair was wet so at least it was a start. She knew now I wasn't going to let her get away with not washing.

But much to my dismay, even after she'd had a shower and put clean pyjamas on, the bad smell still lingered, especially in her bedroom. What the heck was it? It was only later that night as I was sorting through the piles of clean washing to put away that I realised I only had one pair of clean knickers for Ruth. She'd been here five days so there should have been another four pairs of pants. I went to her bedroom.

'Where are your other pairs of knickers?' I asked.

'They're in my drawer,' she said.

But when I looked there was only one pair left.

'I've only got one clean pair of knickers for you from the past five days,' I said. 'I bought you two brand new packs of five. So where are all the other pants?'

'Dunno.' She shrugged. 'I must have lost them.'

It was so frustrating. I went and looked in the laundry basket just to check that I hadn't missed any. As I rooted through that day's dirty clothes, there stuffed at the bottom of the basket underneath everything else was a pair of striped pink pants I recognised as part of the packs I'd bought Ruth. As I fished them out, the smell hit me and I retched. They were soggy, heavy and badly soiled. They were in such a state there was no point in washing them so I put them in a plastic bag and threw them in the bin outside.

Ruth must have been too embarrassed to tell me that she'd soiled herself. I decided not to say anything that night as she was tired. I'd have a quiet chat with her the following day when she got back from the police station and we had a bit more time. But the thought of where the other missing knickers were and what sort of state they might be in preyed on my mind.

The next day when Ruth was at the police station, I dragged the hoover upstairs. I wanted to give her room a good clean to see if that would help to get rid of the smell. I opened the window to let in some fresh air and glanced around. I was pleased to see her bed was made – at least she'd listened to something I'd said. I decided to wash her sheets but as I pulled back the duvet and started to strip the bed, a putrid stench hit my nostrils. I couldn't understand where it was coming from. It was only when I looked down the side of the bed that I found out. Two pairs of badly soiled pants were stuffed down there between the mattress and the wall. I was like a woman possessed now and after a frantic search, I found two more pooey pairs shoved underneath the mattress. I'd got my missing knickers.

For an eleven-year-old to soil herself like this I knew there had to be something very wrong indeed. I had to find a way to handle this sensitively yet firmly.

That afternoon when Ruth got back I had a quiet word with her before Louisa and Lily came home.

'I found the knickers in your room,' I said gently. 'I'm not cross. There's nothing to be ashamed of if you've had an accident. You should have told me instead of hiding them.'

'What knickers?' she said innocently. 'I ain't got no idea what you're talking about.'

'The pants that you'd soiled and then put down the side of your bed and under your mattress,' I said.

'That's nothing to do with me,' she said. 'I wouldn't do something like that.'

She swore point-blank that it wasn't her.

'One of the others must have done it,' she said. 'In fact, I think I saw Lily sneaking into my room the other day. She must have done it.'

I couldn't believe what I was hearing.

'So, you're saying that Lily came into your room, found your clean knickers, pooed in four pairs of them and then shoved them down the side of your bed?'

'Well, I don't know how she did it,' she said. 'I just know that it ain't my fault.'

She was in complete and utter denial.

'Ruth, I'm not angry with you,' I told her. 'I just want you to be clean and comfortable. If you poo your knickers then it doesn't matter, but please don't hide them or put them in my laundry basket.

'You must change them straight away then put on a clean pair and put the dirty pair in the bin outside. Do you understand? They make both you and your room smell.'

'I told you before, I don't know what you're going on about,' she said.

It was exasperating and frustrating. I wanted to help her and try and understand why she was doing this but if she wasn't even willing to admit responsibility then it made it impossible to work with her on this.

If Ruth was going to behave like a toddler then I was going to have to treat her like one.

'Every night I'm going to check the laundry basket to make sure that there are a pair of knickers in there,' I told her. 'If you've had an accident then just tell me. I'm not going to get cross. I just want to make sure that you've thrown them away.'

'I can't believe you're doing this,' she said.

But drastic times called for drastic measures and it was the only way I could guarantee that she was wearing clean underwear.

Even then, some days there were no knickers in the laundry basket at the end of the day.

'Did you have an accident?' I asked her gently but Ruth shook her head.

'If you did I'm not going to be angry, I just want to know where your pants are.'

'I must have lost them,' she told me.

'So you lost them somewhere between the bathroom and your bedroom?'

The next day, I'd search her whole bedroom, desperately looking for where she'd hidden the knickers and I'd always find them rolled up in a ball somewhere and badly soiled.

It was an ongoing battle to make sure that Ruth had a shower every day and changed her pants if she had an accident. Her smell was no longer confined to her bedroom; I had fabric settees in the front room and the stench had started to cling to them. It was driving me mad and neither Louisa nor Lily would sit near her any more.

'Can't you do something about it?' Louisa begged me. 'I can't sit next to her and watch TV.'

'Believe me, I'm trying,' I told her.

I didn't want to isolate Ruth from the front room or embarrass her in front of the others but the message wasn't getting through and she needed to know that it wasn't acceptable for this to carry on. I brought down a plastic chair from my bedroom and put it in the living room. When Ruth came home that day I showed her the chair.

'I don't want to do this, Ruth, but you haven't given me much choice. When you come into this room and you want to watch television with everybody, this is where you'll have to sit,' I told her.

'If you don't want to have a shower or clean yourself properly then that's up to you but it's not fair on everyone else in the house. When you sit on my sofas you leave a smell on them and that's not OK.'

'That's not f**king fair,' she swore. 'You're a b**ch.'

She effed and blinded and eventually stomped out of the room. I felt bad for Ruth but I knew I had to do this as nothing else seemed to be working.

The next day, my supervising social worker from the local authority came round to see me and talk through how things were going with Ruth. Rachel was in her late fifties and had years of experience, so chances were if I had a problem or a situation with a child, she'd dealt with something similar in the past. It was always helpful to run things by her.

I made us a cup of coffee and we went into the front room for a chat.

'Ooh, Maggie,' she said. 'I don't mean to be rude but it's a bit whiffy in here today.'

'Ah yes, that's one of the issues I wanted to get your advice on,' I said, before filling her in on Ruth's hygiene issues.

'It's so tricky because I can't address the real root cause of it,' I said. 'It's all likely to be connected to the abuse and her view of herself but I can't say any of this to her in case it opens up a discussion that might jeopardise a potential court case.

'Plus the other children don't think I'm doing anything about it. They don't know any details about Ruth's past or realise that my hands are tied.'

I explained how I thought Ruth was allowing herself to smell like this to distance herself from other people. I suspected it was also something that she'd done in the past to try and make herself repulsive to her father in the hope that he would leave her alone.

'She's been through a terrible time and I think in her old life she was isolated at home and isolated at school. I think she felt the world had given up on her.

'She doesn't feel worthy enough and this is a way of making sure people keep their distance,' I said. 'It's such a sensitive subject but I had to do something.'

'I completely agree with you,' Rachel told me. 'You've done the right thing introducing the plastic chair and checking where her pants are. You've tried talking to her but obviously the message wasn't getting through and so you can't have her going round smelling like that. Besides, it becomes a hygiene risk for your other children.

'All you can do is persevere and hope that Ruth eventually understands that you're not going to tolerate it.'

I hoped that she was right.

Unfortunately rather than getting better, things got worse. A few days later I was getting some towels out of the airing cupboard. As I reached in to pull the clean towels out, my hand touched something warm and squelchy. As soon as the stench hit my nostrils, I knew exactly what it was and who was responsible. The smell was so intense it made me gag. Nestled between my lovely clean, fluffy towels there was a little package of human stools, loosely wrapped in toilet paper. The boiler was underneath the shelves so it was warm in the cupboard and for all I knew the package could have been festering in there for days.

I felt physically sick as I fished it out and threw it straight in the bin. I put the towels on a boil wash then put my rubber gloves on and got to work disinfecting and scrubbing the whole cupboard.

Despite everything, I wasn't angry with Ruth. I knew that some of this was about control. Ruth had had no control in her life at all – about being abused or beaten or taken into care. She didn't decide what she ate, where she slept or where she lived. The only thing she had control of in her life was when and where she went to the toilet. I also knew that by leaving these little parcels around the house, Ruth was challenging me. She was testing me to see if I would accept her or reject her – as everyone else in her life had done.

'I think it also has a lot to do with self-esteem and how she sees her body,' I told Liz when I called her that day. 'She's disgusted with herself and, in a way, perhaps she's ashamed of her bodily functions so she's trying to hide them.'

There could be a number of reasons why she was doing it but it was tricky trying to address them with Ruth without tackling the root cause.

'I know she can't talk to me but could we get her some counselling?' I asked Liz.

'The police don't want her to talk to anyone until after any potential court case,' she said. 'As soon as the legal proceedings are over of course we'll organise some therapy for Ruth.'

'That's a long time for her to wait,' I said.

I knew she was going to need all the psychological help she could get after what she'd been through.

This time I decided to try a different tactic and not mention the poo parcel in the airing cupboard to Ruth. If I didn't react then perhaps it would be a one-off. However, a few days later I was cleaning the bathroom when I saw a suspicious little package shoved behind the U-bend of the toilet. I got a handful of baby wipes, picked it up and flushed it away. Again, I didn't say anything in the hope that this strategy worked. But a few days later I found another parcel shoved behind the sink and I knew I couldn't stay quiet any longer. I popped my head around Ruth's bedroom door.

'You seem to have left something in the bathroom,' I said casually. 'Can you go and clean it up please?'

She glared at me and stomped off to the bathroom.

'I don't know what you mean,' she sighed. 'I ain't left nothing in there.'

'If you have a look behind the sink near the handwash you'll see exactly what I'm talking about,' I told her.

I didn't wait around for Ruth to question or deny it as I knew she would, I walked away. Thankfully when I checked later, the package had gone. From then on, whenever a poo parcel appeared, this was the way I handled it. Because I didn't rise to her bait, get angry or tell her off, I think Ruth realised that I wasn't going to get rid of her and eventually she stopped.

At last she started to listen. Every night there was a pair of knickers in the laundry basket and Ruth stopped soiling herself. I still had to remind her to have a wash and if I thought she was skipping showers again then I'd follow her up to the bathroom and say: 'Do you want any help?' That was enough to make sure that she washed.

After a few weeks I even started to trust her enough not to have to check the laundry basket.

'I'm so pleased that you're being responsible about keeping yourself clean,' I said. 'But if I start to realise pants are disappearing again then I will go back to checking the laundry basket. Do you understand?'

Ruth nodded and I hoped and prayed that at long last she'd finally got the message and I could put my rubber gloves and bleach away.

FOUR

A Fresh Start

While Ruth was still going to the police station to be questioned, Liz had asked me to sort out a new school for her.

'She can't go back to her old school because her half-siblings are there so we'll have to make alternative arrangements,' she told me. 'We can't run the risk of Ruth bumping into them or her stepmum.'

The local secondary was a twenty-minute walk from our house. Although Louisa went to a different school, several kids in our street went there and I hoped that Ruth might make friends with some of them.

Children under the care of the local authority always got priority in terms of admissions above everyone else and schools were legally obliged to make space for them. The headteacher, Mr Mattison, was more than happy to help when I rang him.

'It's a bit of a tricky situation,' I said, explaining that at the minute Ruth was being interviewed by the police.

'I'll put you in touch with her social worker and she can fill you in on her history if she thinks that it's appropriate,' I told him.

I didn't feel that I should be the one to do that as I still didn't know exact details about the abuse or neglect that Ruth had been subjected to.

'No problem,' he said. 'I'll get the name of her old school so we can get her records sent over.

'Is there anything you can tell me about her?' he asked. 'Has she settled in OK with you?'

'I'm not going to lie to you,' I said. 'She's stroppy and she's got lots of swagger and attitude which is hard to believe when you see the size of her.

'But she's been through a hell of a hard time and I don't think I even know the half of it yet.'

I didn't feel it was appropriate or fair on Ruth to mention the hygiene issues to him and thankfully she seemed to be keeping on top of things. I explained that the police were due to finish their questioning at some point in the next few days.

'Why don't you bring her in and I'll give you both a tour round and then she can start a couple of days later?' he suggested. 'It will give her a bit of a break after the police interviews and a chance for you to sort out the uniform.'

I thought it was a good idea as I knew how exhausted Ruth was. It would give her a bit of headspace rather than rushing straight into the stress of starting at a new school.

'Thanks for being so understanding,' I said.

I knew I'd have to speak to Ruth about starting a new school and I wasn't sure how she was going to take it. She must have been feeling very unsettled at the minute and it was one more thing for her to cope with.

One afternoon when she came home I broached the subject. 'The good news is the police think they've asked you all the questions that they need to ask, so I've been trying to sort out a new school for you to go to. I've found a great one up the road.'

'Why can't I go back to my old one?' she asked.

'Because unfortunately that's where your half-brothers go and the police don't think it's a very good idea for you to see them at the minute,' I explained. 'David has moved to a new school too near to his foster carers and your new school is great. Lots of kids who live in this street go there and the head teacher's a really nice man.'

'Cool,' she said. 'My old school was boring anyway. The social worker said I'd probably have to go to a new one.'

Thankfully Ruth seemed fine about it and appeared to take it all in her stride. I phoned Liz to update her.

'How did she react?' she asked.

'I thought she was going to kick up a fuss but she was absolutely fine,' I said. 'School's a big deal for kids her age and I was worried she'd be upset about leaving her friends.'

'To be honest, Maggie, from what I know about Ruth so far I don't think that she had any friends,' she told me. 'I've spoken to the head and organised for the reports from her old school to go to the new place so at least they'll know if there's anything to look out for.'

The more I learnt about Ruth, the more my heart ached for her. She'd obviously been isolated not only at home but at school too. The poor kid had been friendless, smelly and rejected by everyone. It was no wonder she'd developed this tough attitude – it was her armour to protect herself from the rest of the world.

As expected, the police had finally finished taking Ruth's statement so the following day I went with her for a tour round her new school. Mr Mattison came to meet us and insisted on showing us around himself. He was very informal and chatty and tried hard to put Ruth at ease despite her obvious disinterest. He was a tall man with a deep, booming voice, but he seemed to be a gentle giant.

'This is our brand new library and next to it is the gym where you'll do your PE lessons,' he said.

'Don't like libraries, they're boring,' Ruth muttered under her breath.

'We run a netball club and basketball after school if you're into that sort of thing,' he continued.

'Hate netball and basketball is stupid.' She yawned.

'Sorry, Ruth, what was that?' Mr Mattison asked. 'I didn't catch what you said.'

'Nothing,' she sighed.

Even the new state-of-the-art suite full of computers failed to impress her.

'Ugh,' she huffed. 'Seen it before. We had one of them at my old school.'

Her attitude was embarrassing. Everything she said was negative and she looked totally disinterested and bored. The only things that seemed to vaguely spark her interest were the art room and the home economics area.

'Isn't Mr Mattison a nice man?' I said as we walked out of the school. 'He's really keen for you to settle in and do well.'

'S'alright, I suppose,' she said. 'He's a bit fat.'

And the new uniform certainly didn't impress her. I took her to the school shop in town that afternoon to get her kitted out but she threw a right strop.

'It's horrible,' she said when she tried on the brown, checked, pleated skirt, the brown jumper, blue shirt and tie. 'It doesn't feel right. It's really scratchy.'

'Well, I agree with you that they are not the nicest of colours but I'm afraid the school rules say you have to wear it,' I told her firmly.

I did what I always did with any of my children and bought four full sets – one to wear, one for the wash and two spares in case of emergency. There was also the PE kit, which was a polo shirt and shorts, and she chose a new bag and a pencil case. She was all kitted out and ready for her first day.

The new uniform was on, the packed lunch was made and the backpack was ready – the day that Ruth was due to start at her new school had arrived. Most children starting a new school would be a bit nervous and apprehensive but Ruth was her usual cocky self.

'Good luck,' Louisa said as she left that morning.

'Yeah whatever.' Ruth shrugged. 'It's not like I'm going to need it.'

'It's OK to admit to feeling a bit scared or worried,' I told her. 'It's hard starting a new school in a new place where you don't know anyone.'

'Nah,' she said. 'Don't bother me.'

No matter how hard I tried, I couldn't seem to get past this front that she put up and I never knew what she was really thinking.

At the school reception we were directed straight to Mr Mattison's office. As he came out to meet us, I could see Ruth tense up and for the first time she looked genuinely nervous and vulnerable. He was a big bloke and Ruth looked tiny next to him. The last time we'd seen him, Mr Mattison had been very jovial, cracking jokes and trying his best to put Ruth at ease. This meeting couldn't have been more different.

'Right then, Ruth,' he said in a stern voice as he sat down behind his desk. 'I'm going to lay my cards out on the table here.

'Before you start, I want you to know that we will not tolerate bad behaviour at this school.'

Ruth shrank down in her seat. For once she looked taken aback and was lost for words.

'I want to be clear, young lady, that if you cause any problems in the classroom or disrupt lessons in any way then you will be given time out in isolation. Do you understand?'

Ruth looked close to tears.

'Yes,' she said meekly.

'Yes what?'

'Yes, sir,' she replied.

I must admit I was quite surprised at the change in the way Mr Mattison spoke to Ruth. I couldn't help but wonder what had happened between our last meeting and now to warrant this tough approach.

We were interrupted by a knock at the door and a young woman came in.

'This is your new teacher, Miss Wilcox,' he told Ruth. 'She's going to take you off to your classroom. Now you remember what I've said.'

'OK, sir,' she said sheepishly.

'Have a good day and I'll come and pick you up later,' I told her.

As she obediently followed her new teacher out, she was the most quiet and subservient that I'd ever seen her.

'Gosh,' I said, when she'd left the office. 'You went in all guns blazing there.'

'Well, between you and me, Maggie, let's just say that the reports from Ruth's old school made interesting reading,' said Mr Mattison. 'And with that kind of a pupil we have to start as we mean to go on and let her know that she can't push the boundaries here.

'I won't go into it now as I've got another meeting but I'll give you a call later, if that's OK?'

'No problem,' I said.

I couldn't help but wonder what on earth had been in those reports but I didn't have to wait long to find out. After lunch my phone rang.

'Sorry about this morning,' Mr Mattison said. 'I didn't want you to be shocked by the way I was with Ruth but, honestly, the reports from her old school weren't good.

'She's had all sorts of behavioural problems with both pupils and teachers. There's been a lot of answering back, a lot of causing disruption in the classroom and making it impossible for the other pupils to learn. Lots of fallings-out and fighting with other pupils, both boys and girls. It makes pretty depressing reading. There's not a single positive thing in there.'

He described how Ruth was also behind academically for her age, her reading level was much lower than it should be and she hadn't kept up with homework.

'What about friendships?' I asked. 'Does it mention how she got along with her peers?'

'From what I've read she didn't have any friendship groups,' he said. 'None of her teachers could name one single friend.'

Again it made me feel desperately sad for Ruth. Everyone in her life so far had rejected her, so it was no wonder that she'd made herself as unlikeable as possible to avoid getting hurt any more.

'Reading between the lines, it's clear to me that things weren't ideal at home,' he said. 'The reports say she was always unkempt, smelly and untidy. She would be wearing her uniform but she'd always have some bits missing or she looked like she'd slept in it.

'She's obviously a very troubled girl.'

After hearing all of this, I felt the need to speak up for Ruth.

'The very fact that Ruth's been taken into care suggests that she's been through a horrendously tough time for an eleven-year-old, as I'm sure you realise,' I said. 'I think she feels completely rejected by everyone in her life and her self-esteem is non-existent.

'I agree with you that her report doesn't sound good, but I'd really like her to start with a clean slate.'

'Me too,' agreed Mr Mattison. 'Me too.'

I was relieved that I'd got him on side and I hoped that things would be different for Ruth in a new school.

'You know I'm willing to work with you in any way I can,' I told him. 'I'll support the school the whole way and make sure Ruth is there every day.

'Also, I'd appreciate it if you could keep in touch with me and let me know of any issues that come up.'

I really wanted this to work for her.

'Well, fingers crossed Ruth uses this opportunity to make a fresh start,' he said. 'And I promise we'll keep you in the loop.'

I was really grateful for that. Often a child will come home from school and tell you they've had a good day because they know that's what you want to hear. It's only later that you find out that they've been in trouble or had a hard time with something. I knew I couldn't rely on Ruth to be honest, as telling the truth certainly wasn't one of her strong points.

That afternoon I went to pick Ruth up from school as I'd arranged. She'd eventually walk there and back on her own but she wasn't familiar with the route yet.

'How was your first day?' I asked.

'Great,' she said, much to my surprise.

She reeled off a list of girls who she said she liked and she told me about her 'buddy' – a person who'd been assigned to help her settle in. It all sounded really positive and I was pleased and relieved.

However, it didn't take long for Ruth to make her mark. On her second day I got a call from her head of year.

'I wanted to let you know that Ruth's been disruptive in a lesson this morning so she'll be spending lunchtime in detention,' she said.

'Thanks for the heads-up,' I said. 'What was she doing?'

She explained that Ruth had been singing in class and not stopping when she was asked to and also pretending to drop things on the floor and making a big fuss. She was obviously testing the waters to see what she could get away with and, although a detention on her second day wasn't good, I was pleased the teachers were taking a tough stance.

'How did your day go?' I asked her when she came home that afternoon.

'Fine,' she said.

'Any problems or anything worth mentioning to me?'

'Nope.'

'So there's nothing that you need to tell me about what happened at lunchtime, for example?' I asked.

Ruth stopped and glared at me and I could tell by the angry look on her face that she knew she'd been rumbled.

'Who told you?' she shouted. 'I didn't do nothing wrong.'

'Well, that's not what your head of year said when she called me,' I told her. 'You can't mess about in lessons like that.

'Look, Ruth,' I said. 'School is school and home is home, but if school rings my home then I will also take issue with whatever has happened as it has involved me.

'As it's the first time you've got into trouble then I'll let you off, but next time I won't be as kind. The next time school rings me, your actions will have consequences, so please make sure that doesn't happen.'

'But it's not my fault,' wailed Ruth. 'I was only singing and dropping my stuff was an accident. I wasn't disturbing no one and all the other kids thought it was funny.'

I knew from past experience that children with low self-esteem often set themselves up to be the class clown. When the other kids laughed at her, perhaps Ruth felt that they were accepting her. Acting silly is often a way of trying to win people over or get their attention.

I hoped the message had sunk in that this sort of behaviour wouldn't be tolerated. However, two days later, I got another call, this time from the school secretary.

'I'm just ringing to ask if there's any reason why Ruth hasn't been wearing her uniform for the past couple of days?'

'Pardon?' I said. 'Could you repeat that, please?'

'We wondered why Ruth was coming to school wearing her normal clothes rather than her uniform. If you're having problems getting hold of the school uniform then let us know and I'm sure we can help out.'

I was really confused now.

'I'm having no problems whatsoever,' I told her. 'Ruth has a uniform and when I've dropped her off at school in the morning she's been wearing it.'

'Well, she's wearing jeans and a T-shirt now,' said the secretary. 'When I asked her why she wasn't wearing her uniform she said that's what you'd put her in.'

'Check her school bag,' I told her. 'I bet you'll find her uniform in there.'

It was baffling, but all I could think was that when she arrived at school she must have been getting changed into her normal clothes and then claiming that I'd sent her to school like that. It was another bizarre way of getting people's sympathy and attention and being disruptive.

What constantly surprised me was how such a tiny, meek-looking girl could cause such chaos wherever she went. She seemed to thrive on creating havoc. I hoped that once the school had sussed out her little ruse it wouldn't happen again, so I didn't even mention it when she came home that night. However, the next day I got another phone call.

'Ruth's turned up in her ordinary clothes again but we've checked her bag and this time there's no uniform in there,' said the school secretary, who was obviously getting weary of this saga.

'Well, she went in wearing it this morning,' I said. 'She must have hidden it somewhere.'

I'd had enough of Ruth's silly games and I was determined that she wasn't going to get one over on me. I drove straight up to school with another uniform for Ruth and also a spare to leave with the school nurse.

'Please hang onto it in case this happens again,' I said.

It was at times like this when I wished I could wear a big badge saying 'I am the foster carer and not the parent' as I often felt I was being silently judged for a child's behaviour when I was doing the best I could in the short space of time that I'd had them.

This time I knew I couldn't ignore what Ruth had been up to.

'Why were you wearing your jeans and a T-shirt in lessons?' I asked her that afternoon when she came home.

'Cos you sent me to school in them,' she replied.

'Really, Ruth?' I said in disbelief. 'Did I?'

No matter how many times I asked, Ruth was adamant that I'd sent her out like that. I knew there was no getting past that, so there was no point arguing with her.

'OK, Ruth,' I said. 'From now on, you'll wear your school uniform at all times and if any of it goes missing, the cash to replace it will be coming out of your pocket money.'

'Alright,' she sighed. 'I'll be glad to wear my uniform. It was freezing in that T-shirt.'

Unbelievably she seemed to believe her own lies.

Ruth was constantly testing my boundaries and the school's, seeing how far she could push us. She tried the same trick with the uniform a couple more times but, much to her annoyance, she realised that she wasn't going to get away with it as there was always a spare uniform for her at school to get changed into. She knew the teachers were wise to her little game and would only give her short shrift. They took her straight to the nurse's room and she had to stay in there until she was prepared to put her school uniform back on. Sure enough, she soon grew tired of that game.

I'd kept Liz updated with everything that was going on at Ruth's new school. Ruth had been there a few weeks when Liz came round to have a chat with me.

'I'm worried that Ruth's not settling in,' she said. 'I've got serious concerns that mainstream school isn't right for her. Perhaps it's a more rigid structure and tougher discipline that she needs.'

'What are you saying?' I asked.

'I'm thinking perhaps that a residential school might be a better fit for Ruth,' she said. 'I know you've found her behaviour challenging at home too. Maybe we expected too much of her?'

'A residential school?' I gasped, shocked.

Residential schools are children's homes with a school attached to them. Kids live there permanently twenty-four hours a day, fifty-two weeks a year. I was dead against it.

'I know Ruth is difficult and the reports from her previous school were terrible but I'm confident that things will settle down,' I said.

Ruth was anxious and unstable enough without sending her to a single-sex residential school where a big group of girls are looked after by staff. In my experience these schools often have a high turnover of staff, and Ruth needed individual attention from one caregiver who she could trust. I felt she was far too young to go somewhere like that and that it would isolate her even more.

'What Ruth needs is a secure, stable home life,' I said. 'A residential school wouldn't be right.

'I strongly believe that being in a small family unit is the best thing for her, especially if there's going to be a court case and she has to give evidence against her father. She'll benefit from having people around her to support her.

'She needs quiet and calm, and the security of a routine.'

'I understand what you're saying,' said Liz. 'But if things don't improve and this new school continues to go wrong then we need to have another plan up our sleeve.'

'I don't think this new school will go wrong,' I told her. 'Give it time and I'm confident that we'll start to see a change.'

Thankfully Liz agreed. In the end Ruth did settle down and her behaviour was much better than at her previous school. She loved the home economics lessons and maths, and Mr Mattison said she wasn't too far behind despite all the messing about in the past.

'Give her a couple of months and I'm sure she'll be performing on a par with her peers,' he said. 'She's a bright little thing.'

He kept to his word about keeping in touch and at the end of every week, either he or Ruth's class teacher, Miss Wilcox, would call to update me. Thankfully as time passed there was less and less disruptive behaviour for them to report.

'Well, Maggie, we seem to have nipped it in the bud,' Mr Mattison told me proudly.

We could see the change in Ruth's attitude as well. She seemed positive about school. At mealtimes when Louisa and Lily talked about their day, she started talking about what she'd done at school.

'There's an art competition coming up that I'm definitely going to enter,' she said.

'Oh, we had one of them at our school,' said Lily.

'I doubt it, Lily,' she said. 'They don't do that kind of thing at baby school. You can win a book token in our one so I think it's much better.'

I even hoped that as her behaviour had settled down perhaps she'd start to mix with the other kids and make some friends. However, as I was about to find out, that wasn't going to be easy.

FIVE

Party Panic

The screams and whoops were deafening as twelve excited children crammed into our living room to watch Mr Magic the magician start his show.

It was Lily's sixth birthday and we were having a party for some of her friends from school. Ruth seemed fascinated by the whole thing. She watched the proceedings like a hawk and her face lit up when she saw the big heap of presents Lily's guests had brought her piled high on the kitchen table.

At the end of the afternoon she pulled me to one side.

'Maggie, it's my birthday in a few weeks. Can I have a party like Lily?' she asked.

'I know it's your birthday.' I smiled. 'Liz told me. And of course you can have a party but wouldn't you like to do something a bit different to Lily? Perhaps something a little bit more grown up?'

'Please,' she begged. 'I wanna magician too and I can invite my friends from school.'

I didn't want to disappoint her as she looked so excited, but I didn't think a magic party was appropriate for a twelfth birthday.

'I'm not sure a magician would be right for a big girl like you,' I said. 'What sort of parties have you had in the past?'

'I've never ever had a party before,' she said. 'My brothers did but I was never allowed one.'

'Well in that case I'll try and make sure you have the best party ever,' I told her and she grinned.

Poor, poor Ruth. My heart broke at the thought of her watching her brothers being made a fuss of on their big days but that her birthday went by unmarked.

I thought about it over the next few days and was determined to make Ruth's birthday special. I was a firm believer that kids should be made a fuss of on their birthdays, especially children in care like Ruth who had never really celebrated their birthdays before. It would be a good way of boosting her self-esteem and making her feel wanted for the first time in her life. I was also keen to meet some of her new friends from school who she often talked about.

I sat her down one Saturday afternoon with a pad and a pen.

'Now, I'd like you to do a guest list of all the people who you'd like to invite to your party,' I said.

'Easy,' she announced. 'I want the whole class to come so then I can get loads of presents like Lily did.'

In many ways, Ruth was very childish. She craved the childhood that she'd never had and she also had a fear of missing out on things – so if Lily had got lots of presents from her friends then she thought she was entitled to that too.

'I don't think I could manage thirty children rampaging through the house,' I said. 'How about choosing a few special friends to take out for tea to Pizza Hut and then they could come back here for a sleepover?'

Ruth's face lit up.

'Yeah!' she said. 'I want a sleepover. How many can I invite?'

'How about eight?' I said. 'That's a nice number.'

'Yes,' she said. 'I'm going to choose eight of my bestest friends.

'It's going to be the best party ever!'

I'd never seen her so happy or enthusiastic about anything before. I bought her some pink flowery invites but as she got to work writing them, doubts were niggling at my mind.

Ruth had only been at school a few weeks and I wasn't sure how many genuine friends she had. Was a party really the right thing? But she seemed very confident about who would be coming.

'Jessica says she can't wait to come,' she said. 'And Emily loves sleepovers.'

Jessica and Emily were the names that she'd started mentioning this week. Right from the start at her new school, Ruth had, always been full of talk about her best friends but as the weeks had gone on, a pattern had begun to emerge. She'd mention a girl's name continually and talk about them all the time.

'Lucy's my best friend,' she'd tell me, and it would be Lucy this and Lucy that.

Pleased that she was making friendships, I'd encourage it.

'Why don't you invite Lucy round after school one night for tea?' I'd ask her. 'Or get her mum to ring me and I'll arrange it.'

Ruth would tell me that Lucy was definitely coming back with her and what night it would be but then at the last minute there would be a perfectly good reason why she couldn't make it. Then the following week she would come home talking about a completely different girl who was now her best friend and Lucy would never be mentioned again.

However, Ruth seemed to have no problem picking eight friends and at the bottom of each invite I wrote *Please RSVP to Maggie* and included my phone number.

Ruth seemed really excited.

'I can't wait for my party,' she said, tucking the envelopes into her school bag.

'How did the invites go down?' I asked when she came home that afternoon.

'Great,' she said. 'Jess is definitely coming. Her mum's going to get in touch with you.'

'Good,' I said.

Maybe I'd been too doubting? I'd thought about checking with the school to see if they could tell me Ruth's friendships but I decided not to bother them in the end and Ruth seemed very confident about who would want to come. I booked a big table at Pizza Hut and waited for the RSVPs to come in. However, over two weeks passed and I didn't hear a thing from any of the parents. With under a week to go until Ruth's party, I started to panic.

'I still haven't heard anything from any of your friends' mums,' I told her.

'That's strange,' she said. 'I know Jess is definitely coming. Maybe she's lost the invite?'

'Well, could you get Jess's mum's number from her and give it to me?' I asked her.

'OK,' she said. 'I know she's coming because she said she was really looking forward to it.'

Inside I was worried. Ruth was going to be devastated if none of her friends came. I couldn't risk her sitting there in the restaurant on the day and no one turning up.

'She's going to be gutted,' I said to my friend Vicky when I popped round to her house that day.

'Well, we can all be on standby and come along if you don't think any of the girls from school will,' she said.

So I put together a back-up plan. Vicky said she'd come along with her three foster children and I also invited my friend Heidi who was a foster carer and her two children.

'I've got Jess's mum's number so you can ring her about the party,' said Ruth when she came home that night.

Even having one person from school there would be brilliant. I rang her straight away.

'I'm just phoning to check that Jess can come to Ruth's party this Friday,' I said.

Jess's mum sounded surprised.

'Oh, let me check with her,' she said. 'Can you ring me back another night?'

I rang her again the following evening.

'The party's tomorrow,' I told her. 'So I really need to know if Jess can come. Even if it's just to Pizza Hut and not the sleepover.'

'Oh, I, er,' she mumbled. 'I'm sorry but she's got something else on so I'm afraid she can't come.'

I could tell from her mum's tone of voice that Jess didn't want to come.

'No problem,' I said. 'I understand.'

I saw the look of crushing disappointment on Ruth's face when I put the phone down and I could have kicked myself for even agreeing to a party in the first place. I was annoyed that the parents hadn't even had the decency to respond to the invites. I suppose that was assuming their children had even passed them on in the first place.

'Don't you worry about Jess,' I told her. 'You're still going to have a lovely party. Vicky is going to come with her kids and so is Heidi, and Louisa and Lily will be there of course.'

'OK,' sighed Ruth. 'It's a shame my friends are all busy but Jess did say she had ballet and I think Emma has swimming on a Friday night.'

Somewhere in the back of her head she had a valid excuse for everyone and it broke my heart.

I got straight on the phone to Vicky and Heidi. Ruth had met them both a few times before so they weren't exactly strangers.

'I need you to come and make up numbers at Ruth's party after school tomorrow.'

'No problem,' said Heidi.

The following night we all met up at Pizza Hut and thankfully it went well. Heidi was fostering a baby boy called John, and Ruth absolutely adored him. She got on better with babies than children her own age and she insisted on sitting next to him in his highchair. There were eight children including Lily and Louisa and three adults so there was quite a crowd of us. Much to my relief, Ruth seemed really pleased with it all. Everyone had made an effort and bought her cards and little presents like pencils and pens and nice hair bobbles. She looked genuinely happy as she opened them and, much to my surprise, was very good at saying thank you to everyone. I'd brought a chocolate cake along with us and when I lit the candles and we all sung 'Happy Birthday' she grinned and went bright red. It was at times like that that I got a tiny glimmer of the kind of girl she could be underneath the front that she put up.

The following day was Ruth's actual birthday. I'd bought her a silver bike, which I wheeled into the dining room, and Lily and Louisa had got her a pencil case and a book token. She seemed genuinely pleased and surprised.

'Maggie, it's brilliant,' she said. 'I've never had a bike before. But what if I can't ride it?'

'You can learn,' I said. 'Louisa and Lily will show you how.'

I also had another surprise up my sleeve.

'There's someone else coming to see you later,' I told Ruth.

'Who?' she asked.

'Your brother David,' I said.

Now that the police had finished their questioning, Social Services had said it was OK for Ruth and David to see each other again. I thought that it would be good for Ruth. David was the one constant in her life. Here was a person who knew her and hadn't rejected her and that was very important for her.

I'd spoken to David's foster carer and she'd put me on the phone to him. He hadn't wanted to come to Ruth's party as he was worried it would be all girls, but he'd agreed to come round on her birthday.

'He's going to bring his bike round later and I thought we could all go for a bike ride to the park round the corner,' I said.

'Yeah, great,' she said.

I was surprised at how low-key her reaction was. Ruth hadn't seen her brother for months yet she seemed totally nonplussed about him coming round. All I could think was that maybe they hadn't been that close? When the doorbell went later that morning, Ruth went to open it. But there was no big emotional reunion – there were no tears and they didn't hug or kiss each other.

'Alright, David,' she said casually, like she'd just seen him that morning.

'Hiya.' He smiled.

David was a small, chubby lad who had the same dark, straggly hair as Ruth and a pale face. He looked uncomfortable lurking in the doorway in his scruffy tracksuit.

'Come in,' I said. 'I'm Maggie, Ruth's foster carer.'

'Hi,' he said.

He was polite enough although he wouldn't make eye contact with me. He wasn't exactly chatty, in fact he was a typical monosyllabic teenage boy.

'I bought you this for your birthday,' he said shyly, handing Ruth a parcel.

She ripped it open and smiled.

'It's a Secret Seven book,' she said.

Enid Blyton was one of her favourites so I knew she'd be pleased about that.

Ruth seemed desperate to show off to him.

'Come and see the kitchen,' she said, dragging him away. 'And the telly's massive. Bet your foster carer hasn't got one as big as this.'

She was even more cocky and bolshy when he was around.

'I want a drink, Maggie,' she said. 'Get me a drink.'

'Don't be so rude, Ruth,' muttered David. 'You shouldn't talk to her like that.'

She didn't seem to think that I'd pull her up in front of her brother but I wasn't going to tolerate that kind of rudeness.

'Don't even think about speaking to me like that,' I told her.

Ruth looked shocked. I could tell David had power over her and she wanted to please him.

Later on we all went to the local park. Ruth had never learnt how to ride a bike so she was very nervous but she was determined to master it. Both Lily and David tried to show her.

'Put your foot on the pedal and push off like this,' David told her.

'I can do it myself,' she said.

After a few wobbles, she soon got the hang of it and I could tell that she was pleased with herself.

'Well done, Ruth,' I said. 'You see, your determination paid off.'

Afterwards we all came back to our house for tea. Despite his typical teenage boy awkwardness, David took the time to play dolls with Lily and help her build some Lego. Despite the fact that David and Ruth hadn't seen each other since they'd been taken into care, neither of them mentioned their dad, their stepmother or life at their old house. Even though they weren't perhaps close, I could tell that Ruth was pleased that he'd come round.

'You know you can see each other whenever you want now,' I told her when he'd gone. 'You can ring him at his foster carer's, and she's going to invite you round for tea.'

'Can David come and live with us?' she asked.

I shook my head.

'I haven't got room for any more children, I'm afraid,' I told her. 'All my bedrooms are full now.'

'He can share with me,' she said.

'Older boys and girls, like you two, have to have separate rooms.'

For this reason, it was often hard to place two older children together. At first, of course, Social Services had wanted David and Ruth to be looked after separately so they couldn't discuss their statements or compare notes, and now they were both settled at different homes, they didn't want one of them to face the disruption of moving again.

As Ruth's birthday celebrations drew to a close, I was relieved that in the end it had all gone OK. What had happened with her birthday party showed me that sadly Ruth wasn't able to form friendships or make attachments to people yet. She didn't know or understand the rules of friendship.

Parents' evening at school a few days later only confirmed that. She was slowly catching up academically, which was good, but I was keen to know how she was getting on socially.

'Is she making friends and mixing with the other kids?' I asked Miss Wilcox.

But she couldn't tell me who her friends were. I felt sad that Ruth hadn't even a single friend to call her own.

'She's very bossy and loud and is always acting like the class clown or shouting out in lessons, so I think the other girls don't want to associate with her and risk getting told off themselves,' she said.

It was hard. You can't teach someone how to make friends. All I could do was continue to give her stability at home and hope that one day she felt secure enough to trust people and let down her barriers.

Unfortunately, I knew this was unlikely with a potential court case looming.

One afternoon, while Ruth was at school, Liz came round to update me.

'Good news,' she said. 'The Crown Prosecution Service has decided there's enough evidence to prosecute, and Ruth's father has been charged.'

Liz explained that Ian had already appeared in court and pleaded not guilty, and that because of the seriousness of the offences, the judge had kept him on remand.

'As we expected, that means there's definitely going to be a trial,' she said.

I was pleased that Ruth's father had been charged but angry that she had to be put through the trauma of a trial. I had hoped that her dad would eventually admit what he'd done in order to spare his daughter any more pain and anguish.

'We need to tell Ruth this,' I said.

I wasn't sure how she was going to take it. Liz and I sat her down in the front room when she got back from school.

'What is it?' she asked nervously. 'What's happened?'

'Don't worry, it's good news,' said Liz.

'As you know, the police asked you lots of questions about your dad and you did really well answering them all. Because of everything you said they had enough evidence and your dad had been charged with hurting you.

'In a few months he'll have to go to court and hopefully then he'll go to prison because he needs to be punished for what he did to you.'

Ruth looked angry rather than upset.

'See, I told you he'd done it,' she yelled at Liz.

'Ruth, I've always believed you,' she told her.

'No, you didn't,' she said. 'You made me sit there for all them days, talking to those police people asking me questions. I told you from the start it was true.'

'Ruth, the police had to do that to make sure they had enough evidence to put in front of a judge and to make it more likely that eventually your dad will go to prison for a long time,' I reassured her. 'The police had to ask you all those questions. It didn't mean that they didn't believe you. There's just a process that they have to go through with everybody.'

But Ruth seemed to see Liz as the enemy and was determined to take it out on her.

'What does a trial mean anyway?' she asked, glaring at her.

'It means that your dad has to go to court and you might have to talk to some people about what he did to you,' she explained.

'Can you come to court with me, Maggie?' she asked.

I looked at Liz.

'I'm not sure,' I said.

'Don't worry, Ruth. Maggie will be able to come with you,' Liz said.

'Will I have to see my dad?' she asked.

'No, lovey,' I said. 'If you give evidence, you'll be in a different room from your dad and it will be via a video camera. Don't worry, you won't be able to see him.'

I really felt for Ruth and was worried about the effect a trial was going to have on her. At a time when she needed stability and security, a court case was going to lead to a lot of worry and trauma. Liz took me to one side.

'Now that we know this, I want to make sure that you're happy to have Ruth with you at least until the court case,' she said.

'Of course I am,' I said. 'I'll be here for her and we can support her through it as best we can.'

'Good,' said Liz. 'Then as things progress we can work on a long-term plan for Ruth.

'At least knowing that she's with you for the next few months until the court case will help reassure her.'

But poor Ruth didn't look reassured. She looked absolutely terrified. Terrified of what was to come, about going to court and the possibility of seeing her father again. I wanted her to feel settled and secure, and this wasn't what she needed.

SIX

Challenges

There was a stampede of feet in the hallway as three hungry children ran into the kitchen and sat down at the table ready for their dinner.

Ruth scowled as I put a steaming plate down in front of her.

'What is it?' she asked.

'Sausage casserole,' I said.

She sighed and gave me a look of utter disgust.

'Enjoy,' I said cheerfully.

I hoped that we weren't going to start having a battle over food. Ruth was so skinny and I was trying my best to feed her up. She turned her nose up and made disparaging comments about most of the food that I cooked but then she'd always have a clean plate at the end of the meal.

I dished up Lily and Louisa's portion and then finally a helping for myself. However, much to my amazement, by the time I sat down at the table, Ruth had already cleared her plate.

'Finished!' she announced loudly, banging her knife and fork down with a clatter.

'Goodness me, you ate that quickly,' I said.

I wondered if she'd really been that hungry. Or if, like a lot of traumatised children that I'd looked after in the past, she still had a fear that she wouldn't be given regular meals so she'd eaten it as fast as possible. Whatever the reason, she'd cleared her plate in record time.

'Can I have some more?' she asked.

'Just be patient and wait until the rest of us have finished and then I'll see who wants seconds,' I said.

Ruth gave a sigh of disapproval.

As I tucked into my meal, I could feel her staring at me. Her eyes followed my every move as I lifted my fork up to my lips, took a mouthful and started chewing. Then she did the same to Louisa.

'Is it nice?' she asked, not taking her eyes off her for a second. 'Do you like sausages?'

Louisa was not impressed and looked really uncomfortable.

'Will you stop staring at me?' she yelled. 'I don't like it.'

'I weren't,' said Ruth.

'You were,' said Louisa. 'It's not polite to stare at people when they're eating.'

'I told you, I weren't,' she shouted.

I didn't say anything as sometimes I think it's better to let children sort things out for themselves. Plus I didn't want to tell Ruth off, as that would have caused more upset and done more harm than good. It was uncomfortable having her staring at us while we ate but I could see that she had issues around food that I hadn't quite worked out yet. I hoped it was something that would settle down as she felt more comfortable with us. What I did do from that point onwards, much to her annoyance, was always serve Ruth last.

She seemed to enjoy causing havoc at the dinner table, and soon another issue, quite literally, came up. Aside from eating as quickly as she could, Ruth decided she could also provide more disruption at the table in the form of burping. Everyone burps, but not in the way she did. We were all sitting there eating tea one night and Ruth, as usual, had finished first. She pushed her plate away, leant back in her chair and did the loudest, longest burp possible. We all looked at her in shock, Lily dissolved into giggles and Ruth sat there smirking.

'Ruth, in this house, if you burp please could you put your hand over your mouth and say excuse me,' I told her.

She didn't reply. Instead she let rip with another loud belch. Lily was laughing like mad but she could tell that I wasn't amused. I'm a stickler for children being taught good manners, but I knew this was about Ruth wanting to cause disruption to mealtimes more than anything else.

'That's enough, Lily,' I said sternly. 'Eat up, please.'

I didn't say anything to Ruth in the hope that she would soon lose interest and it would stop, but it was now happening at every meal. It was getting to the point where she was doing it deliberately after every mouthful of food. She had to know that I wasn't going to tolerate that kind of behaviour. Even Lily was fed up with it. It had stopped being funny and it was causing tension at the table. When she belched all the way through breakfast one morning, I'd had enough.

'Ruth,' I said. 'Did you know that in some countries people burp at the end of their meal because in their culture it means that they've enjoyed their food and they're full.'

She was listening but she looked confused. I was talking to her and not telling her off so she was unsure how to react.

'So, do feel free to burp,' I said. 'But if you do, I'll assume it means that you've finished your meal and you're full.'

I knew how obsessed Ruth was with food and having enough of it and I hoped that would put an end to her disruption.

Ruth went back to eating her Weetabix, looking deep in thought. A few minutes later she looked up at me, smiled and did three loud, deep belches.

'Take your bowl to the sink, flower,' I told her calmly. 'You've obviously finished your breakfast.'

'No I ain't,' she snapped. 'I've got a Weetabix left and you said I could have a boiled egg and toast.'

It was the weekend and as we had a bit more time we'd often have a big breakfast with eggs or a fry-up after the usual cereal.

'I want an egg,' she told me crossly.

'Sorry, sweetie,' I said. 'Remember what I said. Feel free to burp, but when you do, I'll assume you've finished and that you're full.'

Ruth huffed and puffed as the rest of us tucked into our boiled eggs. I wasn't worried about her being hungry as there was always a bowl of fruit available at any time for her to eat. I did feel mean but I knew this was less about burping and more about control and power, and I couldn't let Ruth control things. She had to learn that she couldn't sit at our table continually burping as it wasn't nice to listen to when you were trying to eat a meal.

At lunchtime Ruth helped me put the sandwiches on the table. I took the opportunity to remind her of the rules about burping and she looked at me like I was mad.

'I thought that was just this morning,' she said. 'You don't mean every meal from now on?'

'Yes, I do,' I said. 'When you burp, I'm going to assume that you're full.'

Ruth liked to push the boundaries and after eating a few mouthfuls of sandwich, she burped loudly ten times in a row.

'Plate in the sink, now,' I told her firmly.

'But I've got half a sandwich and a yogurt left,' she said.

'Plate in the sink, please,' I repeated and Ruth knew her lunch, although half eaten, was over.

Louisa and Lily had carried on chatting and hadn't paid any attention to her burping. She sat there glaring at us while we finished our lunch and then she stomped off to her room. It was hard and I felt mean, but I won the battle. That was the last time Ruth burped like that at the table.

The burping may have gone but as the weeks passed, it started to become clear that Ruth's issues with food ran a bit deeper than I'd first thought. Because of all the ongoing problems I'd had with her hygiene, I tended to give her bedroom a good clean and hoover at least twice a week. It was a typical messy child's room with clothes hanging out of her drawers, and toys and books on the floor, and although the terrible stench had disappeared, there was always a bit of a whiff about it. It was nothing terrible, it just didn't smell as fresh as I would have liked.

I was doing my regular blitz one afternoon when I pulled out her bed to check for any nasty surprises. After what had happened with the soiled knickers in the past, I always made sure that I looked down the sides of the mattress. There were no pants there this time, thankfully, but stuffed down the side of the bed, in the corner, was a carrier bag.

I opened it up and peered inside. It was full of food and empty wrappers – half-eaten Babybels, empty bags of crisps, an empty packet of ham, cereal bar wrappers, biscuits with bites taken out of them, apples and apple cores. As I rifled through it, I realised that they were all things Ruth must have taken from the kitchen or the fridge. I remembered buying the family pack of ham and the bumper bag of Hula Hoops a few days ago, though I hadn't noticed that they had gone missing.

Why on earth was Ruth taking food and hoarding it? I didn't think she was overeating or had an eating disorder – a lot of the food that she'd taken hadn't even been touched. I wasn't angry with her. I saw it as taking food rather than stealing, and I knew that it came from a place of anxiety. I'd seen this before in neglected kids and as time went on and they felt more secure and settled, and had that stability in their lives, it tended to peter out. I knew I needed to mention it to Ruth to reassure her there would always be plenty to eat, and also to remind her it was unhygienic to have half-eaten bits of cheese and empty food packets festering in her bedroom.

I took her to one side when she got home from school that afternoon.

'I'm not cross with you, I just wanted to have a word about all the empty wrappers and bits of food that I found when I was cleaning your room today,' I said.

'Nothing to do with me,' she replied.

It was the response that I'd expected and I knew there was no use arguing with her as she'd deny everything until she was blue in the face.

'Well, even if it's nothing to do with you, I still wanted to reassure you,' I told her. 'You've seen our fridge and the cupboards in the kitchen. There's always food in them and there's always going to be. We're not going to run out and there will always be plenty for you.'

Ruth looked sheepish for once.

'Ruth, lovey, you don't need to take food and bring it upstairs. Ask me and I'll willingly give you a Babybel or an apple or a packet of crisps.

'Obviously, if you want seven Mars bars or it's right before your tea then I'm going to say no, but don't worry, I promise you, you're not going to go hungry.'

'OK,' she said meekly, giving me a weak smile. 'But I told you it weren't me.'

'If it wasn't you then that's fine,' I told her. 'However, there's still no need to take food upstairs. It creates crumbs and it makes your bedroom smell.'

Ruth was willing to blame anybody and everybody except herself but I only hoped that she'd taken on board what I'd said.

A couple of weeks later we went round to see my friend Heidi. It was baby John's first birthday and she'd put on a little birthday tea. There was all the typical party fare, such as sandwiches, sausage rolls, crisps and the obligatory birthday cake, and we all helped ourselves.

I was busy helping Lily choose her food when Heidi came over to me.

'Maggie, you might want to keep an eye on Ruth,' she murmured. 'She's practically taken half the buffet.'

I looked over to where Ruth was stood in the corner. She had a mountain of food piled on her paper plate that was buckling under the weight.

'You got enough to eat there?' teased Louisa, and all the other children laughed.

'Shut up,' she snapped, her mouth stuffed so full of egg sandwiches that she could barely talk.

'Ruth, that's OK if you're hungry, but don't worry, there's plenty of food so you're not going to miss out,' I told her.

She didn't say anything but looked very uncomfortable. She couldn't cope with seeing that amount of food laid out in front of her without taking it all.

After we'd finished eating we all mucked in and helped Heidi clear away.

'Can you take this outside to the bin for me?' Heidi asked Ruth, handing her a bag full of scraps from people's plates.

I was at the sink doing the washing-up when I saw Ruth walking down the path to the bins at the side of the house. She didn't realise that I was watching her through the window and suddenly she stopped, opened up the bin bag and started shoving handfuls of leftovers into her mouth. I knew she couldn't be hungry after everything she'd eaten earlier but she was stuffing her face. Five minutes later she came back inside but I didn't want to embarrass her by saying anything.

'You've been a long time,' I said. 'Are you OK?'

'Fine,' she snapped.

For the next hour or so the kids all played games while Heidi and I had a coffee. After a while, I realised I couldn't see Ruth.

'Does anyone know where Ruth is?' I asked.

'She was here a minute ago,' said Louisa. 'Maybe she's in the loo?'

But something told me exactly where I'd find her. I wandered through to the kitchen and looked out of the window. It was dark but the porch light was on and I could see a tiny figure outside by the dustbins. The bin was open and Ruth was hunched over it, grabbing food and cramming it into her mouth.

By now Heidi had walked up behind me.

'Poor lass,' she sighed. 'She's a troubled little thing, isn't she?'

'She is,' I replied. 'I don't know how to get through to her.'

I knew from past experience that issues with food didn't just disappear overnight and there was no quick solution. It was something that took months, even years, to resolve and would often slowly disappear as a child felt more loved, safe and secure. All I could do for now was make sure that I kept a close eye on Ruth and her eating habits, and I knew I had a responsibility to flag it up to Liz too.

'I'm not surprised,' she said, when I told her what had been happening. 'When the police were interviewing her she mentioned that meals were taken away from her as punishment for her behaviour, and if she did eat she was only allowed leftovers.

'The other children in the house got treats, like chocolate bars and sweets, but Ruth didn't.'

'Poor girl,' I said. 'It's no wonder she has issues with food.'

I really felt for Ruth. It was heartbreakingly sad thinking of her watching her brothers tucking into regular meals and being given treats while she was left to go hungry. It was pure mental torture. She was obviously taking food because she was worried that she wouldn't be allowed any or that she wouldn't be called down for mealtimes. It related to all her old fears and the things that had happened to her at home. Food had been withheld to punish her and she was terrified that it was going to happen again.

'Keep an eye on it and hopefully it will peter out,' said Liz.

'I hope so,' I said.

From past experience, I knew that food was often an issue with children who have had trauma in their lives like Ruth. Food is often used as a substitute for love and they will overeat to try and get comfort and make up for the lack of care and warmth in their lives. I suspected this was the case with Ruth too. I hoped that as she started to feel more settled, secure and loved then her issues around food and overeating would stop. However, I knew that it was going to take time.

Her anxieties started to show themselves in other ways too. I was putting some clean washing away in Ruth's room when I noticed a top shoved at the back of her sock drawer. It was a navy blue one with sequins on it and I knew it was one of Louisa's. I put everything away myself or handed the kids piles of their clothes so it hadn't got there by mistake.

'What's Louisa's top doing in your drawer?' I asked her. 'Please can you take it back into her room where it belongs.'

Ruth didn't say a word but at least she did as I asked.

But other things started appearing in Ruth's sock drawer too. Lily collected key rings and I found a couple of them in there and a beaded hairband of Louisa's. She must have been going into people's rooms and helping herself.

I already knew that Ruth was what I called a snooper. If I left her in a room watching TV she would think it was OK to go through the drawers, or if she was alone in the kitchen she would read letters from my pile of mail.

Over the next few weeks, whenever I went into Ruth's sock drawer, I'd find things. One of my hairbrushes, a hair bobble of

Louisa's and some lip balm, a little pot of my face cream from the bathroom, a bouncy ball of Lily's. They were silly, insignificant items and they were always in plain view in her sock drawer and not hidden away. It felt more like hoarding than stealing, and I think looking at these objects gave Ruth a sense of comfort. She was so desperate to belong and fit in she somehow thought that if she had other people's possessions then she would be the same as everyone else.

One afternoon, after she'd got back from school, Ruth was sitting at the kitchen table drawing. Alarm bells rung when I noticed what she was drawing with.

'Aren't they Louisa's special pens?' I asked her.

Louisa loved her stationery and she had a big collection of felt-tips, from rainbow markers to pens that smelt like fruit. She kept them safely in her room, but if people asked, she'd allow them to borrow them. However, I suspected Ruth had gone into her room and taken them without asking. Before Ruth even had time to reply, Louisa walked in and I knew there was going to be fireworks. When she saw Ruth drawing with her special pens, she was quite rightly furious.

'Ruth, you're not supposed to take things from my room without asking,' Louisa said.

Ruth shrugged her shoulders.

'They're just stupid pens,' she said. 'It's not like they cost a lot.'

'They're *my* pens, it's my bedroom and you need to keep out of there,' Louisa told her, her voice rising. 'Otherwise, when you get things, then I'll go into your room and take them without asking. And then you can see how it feels.'

I didn't jump in and try to sort it out. Sometimes, as a carer, you need to stand back, as house rules are best taught by the children who live there. What Louisa was saying was completely fair and acceptable, and she seemed to have control of the situation without needing me to step in. In the end, Ruth begrudgingly handed her the pens back.

'Say sorry for taking them,' said Louisa.

But Ruth refused to apologise and Louisa gave her the cold shoulder for the rest of the evening.

Later on, when it was her bedtime, Ruth turned to her.

'Sorry about them pens,' she barked.

'Too late,' said Louisa. 'You're never touching them again.'

After Ruth had gone up to bed, Louisa and I talked over what had happened.

'I wouldn't really take her stuff, Maggie, but she winds me up,' she sighed. 'She's only been here a few months and she struts around like she owns the house. She's even worse when you're not in the room.'

'I'm sure things will settle down,' I told her. 'I know it's hard, but Ruth's going through a lot at the minute. We've got to try and be patient with her.'

I understood how frustrating it was. I knew Ruth was testing us all with her attitude and behaviour.

However, there were certain behaviours that I couldn't turn a blind eye to.

One morning I got a call from Ruth's head of year.

'I wanted to let you know that Ruth came into school today with £20 on her,' she said. 'It all seems to be in loose change.'

I was flabbergasted.

'What?' I gasped. 'I've no idea where on earth all that money that has come from.'

Ruth got £2 pocket money a week and she preferred to spend it on sweets rather than save it.

'We've put it in a bag and we wondered if you'd mind coming up to school to collect it.'

'Of course,' I said. 'That's far too much cash for her to be wandering around school with.'

As I put the phone down, I wracked my brains as to where she might have got that amount of money from. Then suddenly I had a light-bulb moment and my heart sank.

Oh no. She hadn't, had she?

I ran upstairs to Lily's room. On a shelf was her fairy money box. As soon as I picked it up, I knew that Ruth had taken the lot. For the past two years, Lily had been saving up. Every week she got £1 pocket money and if she didn't spend it or she had change from buying some sweets, she popped it into her money box. Any money she got from birthdays or Christmas went in there too and she was saving up for some new Lego. How could Ruth have stooped so low as to steal a six-year-old's savings?

I drove up to school and collected the bag of coins from the school secretary. The only saving grace was that she hadn't spent it and I put it straight back into Lily's money box.

Ruth knew that she'd been rumbled and was going to get a roasting from me when she got home from school. No matter what she'd been through, taking money from people wasn't acceptable. I was sure this wasn't the first time either. Recently I'd gone into my purse to pay for something, thinking I had a fiver or some pound coins, and hadn't been able to understand it when there had just been a few coppers.

I was livid and it took all my strength to speak to her calmly when she got home from school.

'I'm really disappointed in you,' I told her 'It's not OK for you to go into Lily's bedroom and take her money. That's not acceptable behaviour.'

She was unrepentant.

'What does she need all that money for anyway?' she said. 'She hasn't spent it. It's just sat there on her shelf.'

'That doesn't matter, Ruth,' I told her. 'It's Lily's money, not yours. You can't go and take it. That's stealing.'

I suppose in a strange way it was progress in that she didn't try and deny that she'd taken it. But she didn't seem to think that it was a problem and she refused to apologise. Her view was that it wasn't her fault, it was Lily's for having all that money lying around in her room in the first place. It was exasperating and I was so angry and disappointed in her.

However, when I sat down and talked it through with Liz, I started to see the reasons behind it.

'I think it's all about wanting to be the same as everybody else,' I said.

It was about a sense of belonging. Once Ruth believed there was a place for her here in our home and she had that security, I was confident that sort of behaviour would stop.

'Perhaps you need to handle it in a different way,' suggested Liz.

'I think you're right,' I said.

There was no point getting angry with Ruth or punishing her. Deep down, she knew what she was doing was unacceptable. The best way to deal with it was to make her feel that she belonged, that she was the same as everyone else, then she wouldn't feel the need to take things from them.

So I went out and bought Ruth a money box of her own.

'When you get your £2 pocket money on a Saturday then I'm going to encourage you to put a bit of it in there,' I told her. 'Then your money box will be nearly as heavy as Lily's.'

'What's the point?' she sighed.

'You need to save up so you'll have some spending money for when we go on holiday next year,' I said.

I always tried to take the children away somewhere in the UK in the summer. Ruth looked shocked at the mention of a holiday.

'You're not going to take me on holiday with you, are you?' she asked suspiciously.

'Of course we are,' I said. 'We don't know what's happening yet but if you're still here then, of course we'll take you.'

Ruth smiled. It was the first genuine smile I think I'd ever seen from her.

Although I knew there was no point getting angry with Ruth, there was something that I needed to do.

'Ruth, I need to be sure that this isn't going to happen again,' I told her. 'The only way I can do that is by locking the doors in the house. You've given me no other choice.

'My room and Louisa's room will now be locked from the outside as I can't trust you not to take people's possessions.'

Sadly, stealing was something that I'd experienced many times before with foster kids. I'd soon learnt that you could confront the child until you were blue in the face but often the only thing that worked was to remove the temptation. All the bedrooms in my house could be locked from the outside. Lily only had toys, so I didn't think there was any point locking her room every day, but I did ask her to give me her money box for safekeeping. I'd decided not to tell her about Ruth taking her cash as I knew that it would upset her. I didn't tell Louisa about the money box either but I mentioned that Ruth had been stealing.

'The only way to keep your stuff safe is to lock your room when you're out of the house or when Ruth is here,' I said. 'Make sure you take anything from downstairs that's precious to you and put it in your bedroom.

'Sorry, I know it's a pain.'

'I don't mind if it stops her from thieving,' she said.

Much to Ruth's annoyance, Louisa even made a joke of it. One day she put a sparkly hair slide on the side.

'Ruth, I'm putting this hair slide on the table,' she said. 'If you want to steal it, that's fine, but just to let you know that I'll need it back later when I go to my friend's house.'

Ruth didn't see the funny side and stormed off.

It was annoying having to remember to lock my bedroom door. I didn't have many valuables or expensive ornaments downstairs but I discreetly took the giant whisky bottle that we'd been filling with pennies for years upstairs. If anyone came to the house I had to remind them that they couldn't leave anything lying around.

Heidi came over for a coffee one weekend.

'Bring your handbag with you,' I told her when we went from the front room into the kitchen.

When Ruth was in, I had to remember to take my handbag upstairs to my room and lock it in there.

I didn't enjoy having to lock doors in my home but sometimes it was the only way. And that's the way it had to stay until hopefully Ruth got the message.

SEVEN

A Softer Side

If there was one thing that Ruth had a lot of, it was anger. Understandably she was angry about what had happened to her, about being abused, neglected and rejected, and angry about being taken into care. Unfortunately, her way of coping was to take that anger out on everyone else and in particular Lily. Being the youngest and therefore weakest in our house, she was an easy target for Ruth and she tormented her verbally as well as physically. I began to notice that these outbursts always seemed to coincide with a visit from Liz, when she'd come to update us about the legal proceedings.

'Things are still on track for a court case,' Liz told Ruth. 'But I wanted to let you know that it will take quite a long time before your dad has to go to court.'

'How long?' asked Ruth.

'We think it will be at some point in the summer.'

It was December and Ruth had been with us for two months, so that was at least another six or seven months away. Half a year more of worry and uncertainty for Ruth, and I could see it felt like a lifetime to her.

'Can't it be quicker?' she asked.

'I'm afraid not,' said Liz. 'That's how long it takes the police and the lawyers to get everything ready to go to court.'

I could see the fear etched in her face.

'How do you think she's coping?' Liz asked when Ruth went off to play.

'To be honest, not great,' I said. 'She's up and down. Even though the court case is ages away I can tell it's preying on her mind.'

'You know she'll be given lots of support. She'll be talked through it every step of the way, and you and I will be there for her.'

'I've told her that,' I said. 'But she's terrified of seeing her dad and having to give evidence and talk about what happened again.'

'Has she seen much of David?' Liz asked.

'She doesn't seem that bothered,' I told her. 'He's been round for tea once since her birthday but she doesn't ask to see him and doesn't seem that enthusiastic when I suggest organising something.'

'It's best not to push it,' said Liz. 'Perhaps it's too painful for her to see him or it reminds her too much of her father and the past? She'll ask if she wants to see him.'

I truly didn't think Ruth could even begin to move on until after all the legal proceedings were over.

When Liz had gone, I left Lily and Ruth in the front room playing while I went to tidy up in the kitchen. I'd just walked through the kitchen door when I heard Lily scream.

I ran back into the living room to find her in floods of tears.

'She hit me,' she whimpered, rubbing her cheek. 'Ruth whacked me in the face.'

Before I could even ask her what had happened, Ruth jumped on the defensive.

'No, I didn't, Maggie. She's making it up. She's a lying cry baby.'

'You did,' sobbed Lily. 'You hit me for no reason.'

I hadn't seen her do it with my own eyes but I could see that Lily's left cheek was bright red and smarting. Plus she was quite tough and wasn't a whingy kid. She wasn't a complainer or a crier, and would generally get on with things. I cuddled her and tried to calm her down. Meanwhile, Ruth was still insisting that she hadn't done anything wrong.

'Ruth, that's not acceptable behaviour,' I said. 'I know you're angry about what Liz told you today but it's not Lily's fault. It's not fair to take it out on her and I won't tolerate it.'

'I'm not angry,' she shouted. 'I told you, I didn't do nothing.'

'I don't want to hear any more,' I said. 'I can't trust you to be near Lily so please go upstairs to your room.'

'You never believe me,' she yelled. 'She's lying. I ain't touched her.'

The big red mark on Lily's cheek told me otherwise. The poor little lass was shell-shocked.

'Why is she so mean to me, Maggie?' she asked.

'I know it's difficult for you to understand,' I told her. 'But Ruth's going through a hard time. Her daddy wasn't nice to her so she's very cross at the whole world at the minute.'

She was too young to really get it. The fact was Ruth was a fiery ball of anger who caused disruption wherever she went. I knew things were going to get worse rather than better as we got closer to the court case. Understandably, even the thought of giving evidence against her father was making her tense and wound up.

Over the weeks that followed, the situation deteriorated. Ruth was sneaky, in that I never actually saw her hit Lily. She'd always wait until I was out of the room. I'd be in the kitchen or upstairs in the bedrooms doing something and suddenly I'd hear a piercing scream that made my blood run cold. Then Lily would come running to find me, crying and crying, with Ruth following behind her, shouting: 'I didn't do nothing, did I, Lily? I didn't touch her, honest.'

One day it was nipping, the next hair pulling or punching. No punishment seemed to be enough to stop her doing it and I worked out the only way to handle it was to remove the temptation. I couldn't leave Lily in a room alone with Ruth so I'd always have to make up some excuse for one of them to come with me or help me with something, or I made sure I stayed in the room to keep an eye on them both.

'It's exhausting,' I told my supervising social worker when she came round to see how I was getting on. 'I've got to be permanently on my guard.'

'Why do you think she's doing it?' she asked.

'Oh, I know exactly why,' I said. 'She's hurting so she wants to make someone else hurt, and Lily's younger than her so she's an easy target.'

It wasn't just physical abuse either. Ruth was constantly goading her and trying to put her down. Lily loved Lego and she'd spend days building something, then Ruth would come into the room and break bits off it when she wasn't there so it was ruined.

For a six-year-old, Lily really took care with her appearance and she'd take time choosing her clothes and spend ages doing her hair in the mirror. She adored hats so I bought her a straw hat with fake flowers on it. She came downstairs one night to show it off to us.

Ruth was watching the telly but when Lily came in she looked up and frowned at her.

'You look really stupid in that hat,' she said and her face dropped.

'No, she doesn't,' said Louisa protectively. 'Ignore her, Lily. You look great. It suits you.'

Louisa had got to the point where she couldn't stand Ruth. She was polite to her, but she refused to have anything to do with her. Louisa was fiercely protective of Lily and I think she'd seen Ruth hurt her too many times and was fed up with her constantly winding Lily up. Once Louisa had made her mind up about someone there was no changing it, and Ruth had definitely burnt her bridges there. I knew I had to respect her opinion but at the same time stay as neutral as possible as I didn't want any of them to think that I was taking sides. Louisa was old enough to know her own mind and I couldn't do anything to change that.

One weekend Lily was going to a friend's creepy crawly fancy dress birthday party and she wanted to dress up as a spider. I spent weeks making her costume and we all knew how excited she was about it. I bought her a black top and trousers and made eight legs out of old tights stuffed with balls of newspaper that I sewed onto the top. For weeks Lily was talking about this costume and how she couldn't wait to wear it, and I was pretty pleased with my efforts.

On the morning of the party, Louisa and I helped Lily into her outfit and padded out her top with balls of newspaper so her body looked nice and round like a spider's. She proudly came into the living room to show everyone how it looked.

'You look so stupid, Lily,' sneered Ruth. 'You look really fat. People won't believe that's a costume.'

Lily's eyes filled with tears and her bottom lip started to tremble.

'No, I don't,' she said. 'I look good, don't I, Maggie?'

'You look wonderful,' I said.

'Stupid fatty,' sniggered Ruth under her breath.

No matter what we said, Ruth had sown the seed of doubt in Lily's mind. She had a complete meltdown and ripped the costume off.

'I'm not wearing it,' she sobbed. 'I'm not going to the stupid party.'

I was furious with Ruth.

'That was mean,' I told her. 'You've really upset her.

'If you can't say anything nice, then don't say anything at all.'

She shrugged and gave me a sly smile. I was fed up with her spiteful behaviour and the way she was always whispering in Lily's ear, trying to undermine her.

I phoned my friend Vicky whose kids were also going to the party.

'Please can you do me a favour and come round here first?' I asked. 'Ruth's been mean to Lily and she's saying she doesn't want to go.'

Vicky and her children arrived and made a big fuss of Lily.

'What an amazing costume,' she said. 'You're going to be the best dressed there.'

Finally, with her confidence boosted, Lily was persuaded to put her outfit back on and she went to the party half an hour late.

Although I understood why Ruth was behaving in that way, it was hard living with someone who didn't come across as a very nice person and enjoyed causing trouble.

'I'm not your dad,' I told her. 'I'm not going to hurt you, but you need to stop this behaviour.

'It must have been awful for you going through what you did but you can't take it out on everyone else. You've got to stop treating people like this.'

For once, Ruth didn't say a word and she refused to catch my eye.

That told me all I needed to know – she knew exactly what she was doing but she couldn't stop herself.

There were times when I questioned why I put up with this disruptive girl in my house and I often felt like giving up. But I knew I wouldn't – I knew I couldn't. Ruth had already faced so much rejection in her short life. I'd promised that I'd be there for her and support her through the court case, and after that, then we'd see. Social Services hadn't even started discussing a long-term plan yet. None of us could see past the court case, and I knew we'd all be glad when it was over.

In between the outbursts of anger, there were peaceful moments. There were times when Ruth and Lily got on well and played nicely together. It was those moments that kept me going and I clung onto them.

Ruth was quite childish in her play and she and Lily enjoyed doing similar things. One freezing cold winter's day they both begged to go out into the garden. We had a huge sandpit out there that took up practically the whole lawn.

'If you get wrapped up, then yes, you can go outside and play,' I told them.

The sand was damp and their hands were red raw from the cold but they spent ages out there, huddled together for warmth.

I watched them through the kitchen window as they made sand-castles, dug moats, built bridges and made patterns with shells.

Why can't it always be like this? I thought as they laughed and chatted together.

At other times, they would spend hours playing with a wooden doll's house or setting up intricate train tracks all around the house. They got on so well sometimes and I think that's why it was all the more hurtful to Lily when Ruth turned on her.

Ruth's softer side would show through at other times too. Occasionally, she'd let her guard slip and I was able to see how vulnerable she was and how much she was hurting. After she'd had a shower one night she came downstairs with dripping wet hair. I was delighted as it meant that she'd washed her hair for once without me nagging or checking up on her.

'You can't go to bed with your hair sopping wet like that,' I said. 'Let me give you a quick blow-dry.'

'Do I have to?' she moaned.

'Your pillow will be soaking,' I said. 'It will only take a few minutes.'

'Alright,' she sighed.

Ruth sat on the sofa while I got my hairdryer out. I blow-dried her long dark hair in sections and curled it underneath with a brush. She was perfectly still and, although she had her back to me, I could see her face reflected in the mirror over the fireplace. For once she wasn't scowling, her eyes were closed and there was a look on her face that I hadn't seen before – peace, contentment perhaps. She wasn't one for physical contact but I could see she was enjoying feeling the warmth on her head and me running the brush through her hair.

'Tell me if I'm hurting you,' I said, trying to tease out some of the knots.

Her hair was in terrible condition and the ends were all damaged and split.

'I can't remember anyone brushing my hair before,' she said. 'It's nice.'

It was desperately sad to think that a twelve-year-old girl had never experienced something so basic as the feel of someone brushing her hair. It was something that I did every day without thinking to the children that I looked after. It was just a little thing that most of us take for granted, but at the same time was such an important sign that someone cared about you. Little girls especially always loved it when I fiddled with their hair and plaited it or put it in bobbles. It was something so intrinsic to a mother–daughter bond but that yet again signified the neglect Ruth had experienced. At times like this, when Ruth allowed her attitude to disappear, I got a glimpse of the kind of girl she could become. Those moments reinforced my determination to help Ruth, to try to break through her difficult exterior to let out the lovely, gentle and kind girl I knew she had the potential to become. It was those glimpses that kept me going, that gave me hope that one day she would change. It was so unfair that she'd had to go through what she had, but it also frustrated me that she made herself so damn unlikeable and was such hard work most of the time.

'I tell you what,' I said, as I brushed the last few bits. 'I think your hair would look lovely with a few inches cut off it.

'What do you think?' I asked. 'Shall I take you to the hairdresser's one weekend?'

Ruth nodded and smiled.

'I ain't been to a hairdresser's before,' she said, and she seemed delighted with the idea.

Afterwards, Ruth went off to bed. The first few nights after she'd arrived I would always ask: 'Do you want me to come and tuck you in?'

'No,' she'd always bark back.

After a while I was fed up with getting my head bitten off so I'd stopped asking. However, tonight something had changed. I was putting the hairdryer away in my bedroom when I heard a voice calling out to me.

'Maggie?'

'Yes, Ruth?'

'Please will you come and tuck me in?' she asked meekly.

I was taken aback but ecstatic too as it was the first time that she'd actively sought out affection.

'Yes, of course I will,' I told her.

I went into her room where she was lying in bed. I always had to be very mindful and cautious with an older child like Ruth who had been sexually abused. I didn't want to do anything to make them feel uncomfortable so, for example, I would never sit on their bed or give them a kiss unless they asked me to.

I leant down and tucked Ruth's duvet around her.

'Sleep tight,' I said. 'Don't let the bed bugs bite.'

'Night night, Maggie,' she replied. 'Thanks for doing my hair.'

'If you want, I can put it in a plait for you for school tomorrow?' I said.

'I'd like that,' she told me.

Blow-drying her hair was such a normal, everyday thing, but it had obviously been a meaningful moment for Ruth. It was nice to see her softer side for once. I sometimes forgot that she was only twelve and she'd been put through horrendous things that no child should ever be put through. She made herself unlikeable and unlovable because that's what she felt she was.

From then on, Ruth would often come to me with the hairdryer and ask me to do her hair. I'd put it in a plait for her and I bought her some pretty bobbles and slides.

A few weeks later I kept my promise and took her to the hairdresser's. It was interesting taking her somewhere that she didn't know. All her swagger and attitude disappeared the minute we walked in the door and she stuck to my side like glue.

'What would you like done?' the hairdresser asked her.

Ruth was at a loss. She obviously wasn't used to making choices or being asked what she wanted.

'How about a bob?' I suggested. 'Or a just a good trim if you want to keep it longer?'

'You choose,' she told me.

I hadn't noticed this before but I could see she hated sitting in front of the mirror. She didn't like seeing herself in the glass and whenever she caught a glimpse of her reflection, she'd look away. I felt so sad for her but to be honest I wasn't surprised as I knew Ruth had such cripplingly low self-esteem. For the entire appointment, she sat with her head down, staring at the floor. She'd never been so meek and quiet, and I could see her vulnerability.

The hairdresser ended up taking a good five inches off to try and get rid of the damaged hair.

'Look in the mirror, Ruth,' I said afterwards. 'It looks brilliant.'

Although she would only have a quick glance, I could tell she was pleased with it.

The next morning when she got up I noticed one side of her face was swollen.

'Ruth, lovey, is your cheek OK?' I asked her.

'It's a bit sore, I suppose,' she shrugged. 'It hurts in my mouth.'

I took one look at her red swollen gum and I knew we needed an emergency trip to the dentist. A check-up had been on my list of things to do with Ruth anyway. Unfortunately, my dentist was fully booked, but I managed to get her an appointment with a different dentist on the other side of town.

Ruth looked terrified as we waited to go in.

'It's OK,' I said. 'He's going to take a look in your mouth and try and work out why it's swollen.

'Have you been to the dentist before?'

Ruth shook her head. I could see her trembling with fear as she sat in the dentist's chair. He was a nice, polite man but as he looked into Ruth's mouth he started tutting and shaking his head. After he'd examined her, he took me to one side.

'Do you not have toothbrushes in your house?' he asked. 'I'm appalled that anyone can let a child's teeth get in such a state.'

I was shocked at how vicious he was towards me.

'Look,' I said. 'I'm not Ruth's mother, I'm her foster carer and she only recently came to live with me.

'The state of her teeth is nothing to do with me.'

I didn't normally tell people that, but I couldn't bear him judging me. The dentist looked mortified.

'I'm so sorry,' he said. 'Her teeth are in a dreadful state. I can't believe any parent would let them get like that.'

He explained that Ruth's teeth were coated in plaque, a couple needed to be taken out because they were completely rotten and she needed several fillings.

'She's got a nasty gum infection too, which is what's made her cheek swell up,' he said. 'She must have been in a lot of pain for a long period of time.'

I knew from experience how excruciatingly painful toothache was. Poor Ruth had never mentioned it. She'd suffered in silence.

After my outburst, the dentist couldn't have been more helpful. He treated Ruth with such care and gentleness.

'It's going to take quite a few months, but don't worry, we'll get your teeth sorted, young lady.

'You've got to promise me, though, that you'll keep brushing them twice a day.'

Ruth nodded meekly.

Yet again I felt so sad for her. She'd not been cared for or looked after. No one had been bothered if she didn't brush her teeth or wash or brush her hair for days or if she went to school in a dirty uniform. There had been no one on her side looking out for her. She had been treated as a non-person, a ghost, someone who didn't really exist. It was no wonder that she was the way she was. She felt that everyone had given up on her and causing trouble was the only way she could get noticed.

Ruth needed to learn to be part of a loving family and I tried to get her involved in days out and activities we liked to do together, even though she was very resistant at first.

Sometimes on a Sunday we liked to go to markets. We'd get up early and I'd give Lily and Louisa a few pounds so they could buy a few bits and pieces themselves. They loved it, but Ruth dragged her feet.

'Do we have to go?' she moaned. 'It's so boring.'

Afterwards we'd go and meet my friend Marion, who was a foster carer and had four children, for a country walk in the hills. We'd take a picnic with us and the kids all ran free, playing games of football and hide and seek, and sometimes we'd stay up there all day. Of course, Ruth hated it.

The first time we went she refused to get out of the car.

'Don't like it,' she said. 'It's freezing. Why are we up here?'

'Well, the others want to go,' I said. 'So you'll have to stay in the car.'

I could only guess that she was anxious about mixing with the other kids. Ruth was stubborn, though, and, sure enough, she kept to her word and sat in the car for two hours, staring out of the window with a sulky look on her face.

'Is she OK?' Marion asked, as she glared at us.

'Oh, she's fine,' I said. 'She has to learn to fit in with family life and get on with it like everyone else.'

After a few weeks, Ruth gradually started to warm to the idea. She came out of the car and began joining in with the other kids. After a few months, going walking in the hills became her favourite thing to do and she was always asking me about it.

'Are we going up to the hills this weekend?' she asked. 'Is Marion coming with us?'

I couldn't believe it when she even offered to help me make the picnic. I showed her how to make a quiche and she quickly learnt how to chop veg and crack eggs, all the while chatting away to me.

'I've got an idea for when we go up to the hills tomorrow,' I said. 'How do you fancy having a go at making kites?'

Ruth's face lit up.

'Yeah,' she said. 'That would be brilliant.'

The next day we met up with Marion. As we walked from the car park to the top of the hill, I felt Ruth loop her arm through mine and she bounced happily along next to me. It was lovely to see her actively seek out physical affection from me and it made me feel good too, like I was getting through to her and doing something right. Like I'd promised, I'd brought some garden canes and brown paper, and I helped the kids make kites. While they tried them out, Marion and I sat on a bench and shared a flask of tea.

It was a sunny winter's day but the wind was strong up there and the kites took off easily. I watched Ruth, a huge smile on her face, throw hers up into the air. She leapt about, whooping and cheering as it took off.

'It's nice to see her like that,' said Marion.

'It is, isn't it?' I said.

These moments were few and far between but it was lovely to see Ruth forgetting her troubles and her worries and just enjoying being a child. Her attitude and swagger had gone and she looked carefree.

It gave me hope that one day, when the court case was over, perhaps she could break free from her past and move on. Perhaps she could be happy for the first time in her life.

EIGHT

Memories

Christmas had crept up on us. Ruth had been with me for nearly three months and with just a few weeks to go, there was something I knew I needed to tackle.

'Right, kids,' I said. 'We need to sort out some of these toys.'

Lily groaned. She knew it was mainly her job as Louisa was older and didn't really play with toys any more.

'Do we have to, Maggie?' she asked.

'Lily, you know that Christmas means lots of lovely new toys from Santa. That's why we need to sort out the old ones and make some space.'

Ruth and Louisa agreed to help her sort through the toys and decide what needed to go up into storage in the loft. I very rarely gave toys away as I never knew what age children I would be looking after at some point in the future.

As I got some cardboard boxes ready to put things into, I listened to the three of them chatting away as they sorted through the toy cupboard.

'Do you get lots of toys at Christmas, then?' Ruth asked Lily.

'Oh yeah,' she said. 'Santa brung me loads and loads last year.'

'And you get to keep them all?' asked Ruth. 'Nobody takes them away from you?'

'Course they don't,' said Lily. 'You get to keep all of them. They're your presents, silly.'

I was listening in to this conversation intently and was about to step in when Louisa asked exactly what I was about to ask.

'Why are you asking that, Ruth?' she said. 'Didn't you get to keep your presents at your old house?'

'No,' she said sadly. 'Well, I was allowed to keep one but Mum took my others away because she said I didn't deserve them.

'But then she gave them to my brothers, and they played with 'em, just not me.'

Lily looked horrified.

'That definitely doesn't happen here,' said Louisa. 'Maggie would never take away your presents.'

'Er, well, she did take away my selection boxes one year,' said Lily.

'Lily, that's because you got four of them and she didn't want you to eat them all at once,' laughed Louisa. 'They were only in the kitchen and you got them back whenever you wanted some chocolate.'

'Yeah,' she said. 'You're right. We don't get our Christmas presents taken off us in this house.'

Poor Ruth. Had anything nice or good ever happened to her in her old life?

There were other moments when we'd glimpse what it must have been like at home for Ruth. She was helping Louisa wash the dishes after tea one night while Lily and I dried up.

'This reminds me of being at my house,' she said.

'Did you often do the washing-up?' I asked.

'I had to do it all the time,' she said.

'Someone else must have helped you?' I asked, but Ruth shook her head.

She reeled off the list of jobs that she'd had to do every day at home, like folding the laundry and making the beds.

'I had to check the boys' bedrooms were tidy, but if they weren't and they were a mess, then I had to do 'em,' she said.

I could tell by the way she talked about it that Ruth thought it was entirely normal that she had to do most of the housework. But to the rest of us, it sounded as if she was little more than an unpaid cleaner.

'Why don't you make me do more jobs, Maggie?' she asked. 'Cos I don't mind. I know how to do things.'

'You do enough,' I said. 'You help me when I ask. If I make tea then all I ask is that you girls help me to clear up afterwards.

'The best thing you can do for me is make sure that you keep yourself and your room nice and clean.'

It made me wary of asking Ruth to do anything, as I wanted her to know that how she'd been treated at home wasn't normal behaviour. However, it had obviously been drummed into her over time.

I can't bear untidiness and one day I lost my rag as Lily had been playing with the Playmobil, Lego and Duplo and had mixed it all in together. I picked up all three boxes and tipped them out over the living-room floor, determined to sort it out.

Ruth immediately came rushing over and started to tidy it up.

'You don't have to do that,' I told her. 'It was my decision to tip it all out. You don't have to help.'

I could see that it was something she'd done automatically and she was fearful of what would happen if she didn't do it.

'I'm not going to be cross with you if you don't help,' I said.

'Was it the same for your David?' I asked. 'Did he have lots of chores to do?'

'He didn't have to do nothing,' she said. 'Neither did the other kids. It was just me.

'Mum said I had to do everything as that was my punishment for being bad.'

As the weeks had gone on, we'd seen less and less of Ruth's brother David. At first, Social Services had set up contact between them but as they were twelve and fifteen now, it was decided to leave it up to them when they wanted to see each other, and David's foster carer and I would sort it out.

'Do you want David to come round?' I'd ask Ruth, but she didn't seem that bothered.

He might have been her brother but for two children who had grown up in the same house, they couldn't have been more different. David was confident and had lots of self-esteem. He was doing well at school, had lots of friends and, by all accounts, had settled in well at his foster carer's. He was relatively unscathed by the past, compared to his damaged, angry, neglected little sister. I don't think Ruth liked being around him because it reminded her of being at home and the abuse that she'd suffered at the hands of their father.

'Do you want David to come round on Christmas Day?' I asked her.

'I don't really mind.' She shrugged.

They swapped presents in the run-up to Christmas but they didn't seem to want to be together over the festive period so I didn't force it.

Like all the other kids, I could see Ruth was excited about Christmas but there was also an element of anxiety. On Christmas Day her face lit up when she walked into the living room and saw the carpet covered in presents.

'Wow.' She grinned. 'Are these all for us?'

'Yes.' I smiled. 'And that pile over there is for you.'

Louisa and Lily had already started ripping into their presents. Lily whooped with delight as she saw her new Lego set and Barbie doll and Louisa seemed pleased with the clothes and CDs I'd chosen for her. Ruth sat back and watched them for a bit but didn't start opening hers. It was almost like she didn't quite believe it.

'Go on, Ruth, open yours,' said Lily. 'Let's see what you've got.'

Very slowly and carefully she pulled the wrapping paper off the biggest parcel.

'Oh cool, an art set.' She smiled

To my relief she seemed just as chuffed with the roller boots that I'd bought her.

'Can I really keep them?' she asked me in the same breath. 'All of them?'

'Of course you can, silly,' I told her. 'They're your Christmas presents.'

She seemed genuinely delighted with everything that I'd bought her, but I still don't think she was convinced that they weren't going to get taken away from her. The present that she loved the most had cost the least – a big pad of stickers with her name on. I'd come up with the idea especially to stress the fact that these were her presents and I thought if they had her name on, it would help reassure her that nobody was going to take them away from her.

'Now you can put a sticker on everything that you've got for Christmas and everyone will know that it belongs to you,' I told her.

She smiled and I hoped it had finally reassured her that the presents were hers to keep.

After Christmas, the kids were always allowed to keep their gifts in piles downstairs in the living room for a few days before they had to sort them all out. However, every day Ruth would have the same routine. Instead of putting her presents in a pile like the others, she'd line them all up and count them.

'Ruth, why do you keep doing that?' Lily asked her.

She didn't answer but I knew why.

She was checking to see that they were all there and that none of them had been taken. No matter what we did, it was hard for her to break free from her old insecurities. I knew at home she'd been stuck in a vicious circle of behaviour – she'd behaved badly, a reaction against the abuse, and so she'd been punished and treated badly. She was given nothing good, so she gave nothing good back.

After Christmas, I took Ruth shopping in the sales for some clothes. As she hadn't come with any clothes, I didn't know what she'd been allowed to wear before. But everything she picked up in the shops, I didn't think was appropriate.

'Ooh, look, Maggie, these are nice,' she said, showing me a lacy crop top and some hot pants.

'Ruth, you're twelve not twenty,' I said. 'I don't think they're suitable for a girl your age.'

She seemed to want to wear skimpy skirts and nasty nylon blouses that were much too old for her. I didn't want to get into an argument so I decided to cut the clothes shopping short.

'Look at the time,' I said. 'We'd better go as I've got to take a parcel to the Post Office and I don't want to miss the last post.'

As we drove out of the town centre, I spotted a Post Office so I pulled up outside it. It was on a parade of shops on the opposite side of town to where we lived so I'd never been in there before.

There was a big queue so Ruth and I joined the back of the line. I was standing there when I felt someone staring at us. I glanced around and saw a woman flicking through some birthday cards at the back of the shop. When I caught her eye, she quickly looked away but I knew it was her who had been staring at us.

Did I know her?

I didn't think so. She had short, dyed blonde hair and a rough-looking face. As the queue got shorter and we moved closer towards her, she caught my eye. Then suddenly she put her head down and quickly walked past us and out of the shop.

I felt Ruth tugging at my sleeve.

'Maggie,' she whispered. 'Did you see that woman? That was my mum.'

'What?' I said, surprised. 'Who was your mum?'

'That blonde lady who walked past us just then. That was my mum.'

'You mean your stepmum Marie?' I asked, but Ruth scowled. She still hated anyone referring to her as that.

'Sorry,' I said. 'You mean the lady you lived with?'

She nodded.

'I can't believe she didn't even say hello to me,' she said.

That's why she had been staring at us. She'd obviously been shocked when she saw Ruth.

'Are you OK?' I asked Ruth, and she nodded, although she looked in shock.

After that, Ruth was very clingy and didn't leave my side. As we walked out of the Post Office and back to the car, I noticed her looking around nervously.

'Don't worry,' I told her. 'She can't hurt you. It was obviously a shock for her to see you too and I bet she's long gone now.'

But Ruth didn't relax until we were back in the safety of our car.

Although her stepmother would have been told by Social Services and the police that she wasn't allowed to contact Ruth, I would have thought that if she'd bumped into her by chance she would have still said hello. Over all the years I've been fostering, it's only happened one other time that a child has bumped into a family member that they've been removed from. On that occasion, the relative did say hello to the child and thankfully there wasn't a big scene. I've found the best way to deal with those types of tricky situations is to say hello if they want to and if the child seems calm. I'm always polite but make a quick exit.

That night I made sure I put it down in my daily notes.

A woman was staring at us strangely in the Post Office.

She didn't say anything to us but after she'd gone past Ruth told me that the woman was her stepmother Marie. Ruth was nervous and on edge afterwards.

'How did Ruth seem afterwards? Liz asked when she next came round.

'I think she was a bit shaken up to see her and she asked me later on if her brothers were still living with her stepmum,' I told her. 'I said I wasn't sure but that I thought they were and I reassured her that her dad was definitely still in prison and they were going to keep him there until the court case.'

'It's funny you should mention Marie as there's something I wanted to tell you,' said Liz.

'Unfortunately, the police have decided not to pursue charges of neglect against her.

'The CPS has said it would be difficult to prove as it's basically Ruth's word against hers. All the other children in the house were well cared for and clean, and Ruth would be painted as bit of a troublemaker.'

It was disappointing but I understood the argument. Having lived with Ruth for over three months, I knew what her behaviour could be like and it wouldn't be hard to paint a picture of a troubled, rebellious girl. Thankfully, we hadn't told Ruth about any possible charges against her stepmother. We had to put that behind us and focus on our main battle – convicting her father for all the terrible things that he'd done to her.

A few weeks into the new year, an old nightmare came back to haunt me. I was cleaning Ruth's room one day when I was struck by an overpowering smell.

Oh, God, not again, I thought.

I opened the windows and set about trying to find the source. First of all, I pulled her bed away from the wall. There wasn't any food shoved down there or, thankfully, any soiled knickers. But no matter what I did, I couldn't work out where this smell was coming from. It was a strange, stale, musty stench that I couldn't put my finger on. I looked in the wardrobe and drawers, and underneath the bed, and I took all the sheets off in case she'd wet them. It was driving me mad and I was considering trying to lift up the carpet when I noticed something. Someone had made a small slit down the side of the mattress. Gingerly, I put my hand inside, not daring even to guess what I was going to find. To my horror, I pulled out a used sanitary towel.

'Oh, Ruth,' I sighed, 'what on earth have you been up to now?'

I went and put my rubber gloves on, and fished out nine or ten more soiled pads that had been shoved in there. It was unpleasant but I wasn't angry with Ruth, and I knew I needed to handle this gently. It was a bit like the poo parcels that she'd left around when she'd first moved in with us. She was ashamed of anything to do with her body and her bodily functions. When Ruth first came to me Liz had told me that she'd recently started her periods and I knew that would have been especially traumatic for her as it signified becoming a woman and was connected to sex and having babies.

When Ruth had first moved in I'd shown her where I kept the boxes of pads and the nappy bags to put the used ones in, as they couldn't be flushed down the loo. In fact, they were in the same cupboard where she'd hidden her first poo parcel. I decided to have a quiet word with her when she got home from school but not make a big deal of it.

'Ruth, lovey,' I said. 'Why on earth have you been putting used sanitary towels in your mattress?'

She looked embarrassed and for once she didn't deny it.

'I didn't know what to do with them,' she said.

'Then you should have come and asked me,' I told her.

I took her to the cupboard and showed her where the bags were, next to the sanitary towels.

'When you want to get rid of one, pop it in a nappy bag and then put it in the bin outside,' I told her.

'OK,' she sighed.

The towels hadn't been there that long but it had been enough time for the rancid smell to permeate into the whole mattress and I had to buy a new one. This time I wasn't prepared to take any chances. I bought two waterproof sheets and painstakingly sewed them together so the mattress was encased. It meant it was completely protected and if Ruth made another slit in it then I'd soon see the rip.

However, despite our little chat, Ruth continued to hide used sanitary towels in her room. I'd check the bin each day and there would be no nappy bags in there.

'Ruth, we can't go on like this. You're creating a health and hygiene risk,' I told her. 'If I can't trust you to dispose of your used pads then I'm going to have to do it for you.

'I'll keep the pads in my room and I'll put the bags in the bathroom. When you need a new pad you come and tell me, and give me the used one in the nappy bag and I'll put it in the bin outside.'

I could tell Ruth wasn't happy about it but she begrudgingly accepted that this was the way it had to be. Like the knickers, all I could do was take control and do everything for her until she got the message. I really felt for her, and I hoped the court case and counselling would help her resolve some of her self-esteem issues. But, until then, a bit of tough love was all I had, as I couldn't afford to keep replacing mattresses.

Because of the way she'd been treated at home, Ruth had a warped view of herself. No one had cared for her so she didn't care for herself. I wanted to show her that now she was somewhere people did care, but she found that difficult to cope with at first.

I often picked up bits and pieces for the kids when I was out and it was something I did without thinking. As it was winter, I came home one day with a stick of lip balm for each of the children to keep in their pockets at school in case their lips were dry.

'Why've you got me that?' Ruth asked suspiciously.

'Because I wanted to,' I said. 'Because I like you and I care about you.'

Her face screwed up into a frown.

'I got one for you and Louisa and Lily so your lips don't get dry in the cold weather.'

'Oh,' she said, unsure what to say.

I noticed her hands were dry and sore, so another day I bought her home some hand cream from the supermarket and a little pot to keep her bobbles and hair slides in. Another week I got her a smelly body spray from the chemist's and a little notebook that I saw and thought she'd like. They were small, inexpensive things but I hoped they'd help make her feel cared for and loved, that she was no longer a ghost girl but a real person who deserved to be treated with kindness and respect.

Now we knew Ruth would be staying with us for a while I wanted her to feel at home in our house and my thoughts turned to her bedroom. The room was painted neutrally, and had cream curtains and a mirror on the wall. It was clean and tidy but I wanted to personalise it.

At teatime that night I started a conversation about favourite colours, in the hope I could get a few clues from Ruth.

'My favourite colour is red,' said Louisa.

'I like yellow,' said Ruth.

'Well, I like rainbows,' said Lily, which annoyed Ruth no end.

'You can't have that, it's seven colours,' she told her.

'I can if I want,' she snapped.

There was a set of bunk beds and a single bed in Ruth's room so it looked quite crowded. I'd originally put three beds in there as sometimes I did emergency placements, and a family group consisting of several kids might come in, and it saved time having the room already set up. Now it was going to be Ruth's room, I decided to dismantle the single bed and keep the bunk beds, just in case Ruth ever made friends and wanted to have them round for a sleepover.

I bought two yellow-coloured duvets in a sale and some blue cushions. I also found a nice yellow lamp and a little yellow jewellery box to put on top of her chest of drawers.

I wanted to surprise Ruth so I made the changes one day while she was at school.

'I've got you a new duvet cover and some bits for your bedroom,' I told her on the way in that morning.

'What are they like?' she asked.

'It's a surprise,' I said. 'You can see them when you get home from school.'

I didn't want to give too much away but I wanted to let her know that I was going to be in her room as it was her private space.

My friend Vicky had promised to pop in later and give me a hand dismantling the bed, and the rest was easily achievable for when Ruth came home. Vicky arrived at ten with armful of posters that her kids had decided that they no longer wanted. One was of a ballet dancer in a purple leotard and another was of a view through a window of animals in the distance and beautiful rolling hills.

'These will be great to liven up the walls,' I said.

I even had two Ikea frames that fitted them both perfectly so I was really pleased.

Vicky and I were soon hard at work and by 2 p.m. the room was done.

'It looks lovely,' said Vicky, admiring our handiwork.

It looked fresh and clean and, although it was girly, it wasn't too babyish or over the top. The single bed was now in bits in the loft so the room looked much bigger and I'd found a cream rug for the floor.

'I hope Ruth will be pleased,' I said.

I couldn't wait to see her face when she got back and saw her new yellow palace. When she came in, I didn't say anything as I wanted her to discover her new room for herself so it would be more of a surprise. Louisa was out and Lily was busy playing Barbies. After Ruth had had a drink and some toast, she went upstairs. I followed close behind her, pretending to put some clean towels in the airing cupboard, so that I could hear her reaction. Ruth went into her room. She didn't say a word, but a few seconds later she marched to the door and slammed it shut.

That hadn't been what I was expecting.

'Are you OK in there, Ruth?' I asked, knocking on her door. 'Can I come in?'

'Go away,' she shouted. 'I hate you!'

I couldn't understand it. When she'd got in she'd seemed fine. She'd chatted about her day and advised Lily about what outfit her Barbie should wear. Surely it couldn't be the new room that had upset her?

'Ruth, if I've done something to upset you then we need to talk about it,' I told her.

I knocked again and opened the door. Ruth was sitting in the corner of the room, curled up into a ball, sobbing. She didn't look at me.

'I hate you,' she cried. 'You're just like my mum. I hate you.'

'What do you mean?' I asked her. 'What have I done?'

But she wouldn't look at me. I was confused by how upset she was and I couldn't for the life of me understand what had caused it.

I sat on the end of the bunk bed and waited. After a while she lifted her head up. Her eyes were red and puffy.

'Why did you get rid of my bed?' she asked. 'Will I have to sleep on the sofa again? You said it would be different here.'

I went over and sat on the floor next to her. I was heartbroken that Ruth would even think that I would do that to her. I could have kicked myself for taking down her bed and not thinking things through properly and understanding how deeply her past still affected her.

'Of course you've got a bed,' I said. 'I would never expect any child in my house not to have a bed to sleep on or to have to sleep on the sofa downstairs.

'Who do you think the bunk bed is for?'

'I don't know,' Ruth snivelled. 'For more kids that are coming in to be fostered?'

I shook my head.

'No,' I said. 'While you're with me, this room is for you and you only.

'I was trying to make your room look nice and make it special for you,' I said. 'I took the single bed down and left the bunk beds so that when you make friends at school you can invite them for a sleepover if you want to.'

'I can really do that?' she asked.

'Yes, of course you can,' I said. 'Just like Lily and Louisa do with their friends.'

Ruth gave me a weak smile and I handed her a tissue from my pocket to dry her eyes.

'Now you've got to decide which bunk you want,' I said.

'I think I'll sleep in the bottom one so I can turn the lamp on and off easily,' she told me meekly, her ragged breaths slowly calming down.

We sat there for a little longer.

'Why don't you go and wash your face and then let's pretend that you're seeing your new room for the first time, eh?' I said. 'And remember, there's no sleeping on sofas in my house.'

'Yes.' Ruth smiled, jumping up.

She was just coming out of the bathroom when I heard a key in the lock and Louisa walked through the front door.

'Louisa, Louisa, come and see my new bedroom,' Ruth called out to her.

She came upstairs and we all went in and Ruth pointed out all the new things to her. Louisa, bless her, made all the right noises.

'Oh, wow, it's really nice,' she said. 'I love the yellow and it looks much bigger with just the bunk beds in here.'

'I'm going to sleep in the bottom one,' Ruth told her.

I left the two of them chatting and went downstairs to make myself a cup of tea. I needed one after all that drama. I was cross with myself for causing so much upset and not thinking it through properly. But I hadn't thought that moving the single bed would have triggered such a response from Ruth. I felt awful about upsetting her but I'm only human and I don't always get it right. All I could do was remember for the future that transforming children's rooms without their input isn't always the best idea. By dinner time, Ruth was fine and seemed really pleased with her new bedroom, but it was definitely a harsh lesson learnt for me. Sometimes fostering is about taking one step forward and two steps back. Ideas that you have don't always work but you have to learn from them and move on. I definitely learnt an important lesson that day.

NINE

Keeping Mum

When Liz phoned up one day and said she had some important news, I knew something major must have happened. She insisted on coming round to see me in person when Ruth was at school.

'There's been an update I thought you might be interested in,' she said. 'We've managed to track down Ruth's biological mum Sharon.'

'Wow,' I said. 'How did you find her?'

'It turns out that Marie had been in contact with her, on and off, over the years,' she said. 'When Ian was arrested, and Ruth and David were taken into care, she got back in touch with her to let her know.'

'How did she seem when you spoke to her?' I asked. 'Was she shocked?'

'She's distraught,' said Liz. 'Understandably, she was devastated to hear what had happened to Ruth and that her two children are now in care.'

'I'm not surprised,' I said.

Liz explained that Sharon was keen to get back in touch

with Ruth and David. With Ian in prison on remand, she now had parental responsibility for them. She hadn't abandoned the children, because she'd left them with their dad, and she hadn't been living with them when the abuse occurred so she had a legal right to see her children if she wanted to.

'She's made a new life for herself in a village in the middle of the countryside about three hours from here,' said Liz. 'We've made contact with the local authority in her area and they're going to send a social worker round to have an initial chat. Then we'll have more of an idea of her situation and whether we can think about reintroducing her to the kids.'

I was pleased and also curious to find out more.

'I'll let you know when I have any more info,' said Liz. 'Obviously, in the meantime, don't mention any of this to Ruth.'

'Of course not,' I said.

A few days later, Liz came round again.

'A social worker went round to see Mum and it all sounds very positive,' she said. 'She's got a full-time job and her own house, which was clean and tidy, and on the face of it she seems stable with no obvious issues.'

'Does she have a husband or a partner?' I asked.

'Nope,' said Liz, 'She's single and never remarried or had any more children.

'Apparently she's very keen to see Ruth and David but the social worker explained to her that she needs to prove her commitment to the children before we do that.'

Ruth especially was highly vulnerable. If they reunited her with her mum and then she disappeared again, it would do more harm than good.

'As you and I know, Ruth's already faced enough rejection

in her life,' I said. 'I can't put her through any more. I don't think she could take it.'

'Whatever happens, we wouldn't introduce them until after the court case,' said Liz. 'Ruth's got enough on her plate with that coming up.'

That was a relief. I didn't think Ruth could cope with any more emotional upheaval right now. None of us knew how she would react to knowing her biological mum was back on the scene and we couldn't risk jeopardising the court case.

'I also wanted to ask you something,' said Liz.

She paused.

'I wondered if you'd be prepared to come with me to meet Sharon? I don't want to sugar-coat things about Ruth for her.

'I can read her the reports but you're the best person to tell her about Ruth and her behaviour and what she's like.

'She needs to know the full picture before she decides whether she wants to get back in contact or not.'

'Of course,' I said.

A few days later, without breathing a word to Ruth, I got my friend Heidi to help with the kids, and Liz and I went to see Sharon. I was curious about meeting her and I wondered if she would be like Ruth.

'What's she like?' I asked Liz as she drove me there.

'She sounds nice on the phone,' she said. 'Very polite and quietly spoken.'

'Totally different from her daughter then,' I said, and we both smiled.

'I don't know what you think, but I've brought along some recent photos of Ruth,' I told Liz. 'I thought her mum might like to see them.'

'Good idea,' she said. 'Let's see how it goes, but definitely ask if she'd like to see them. I bet she'll be delighted.'

A few hours later we pulled up outside Sharon's terraced stone cottage in the middle of a pretty village. The front garden was tiny but neatly kept.

Liz rang the bell and eventually a woman came to the door.

'Sharon?' Liz asked.

'Hello,' she said nervously. 'Come on in.'

What struck me as she showed us in was how much she looked like Ruth. They had the same long dark hair, pale face and big eyes. But that's where the similarity ended. Unlike Ruth, she seemed meek and mousy. She was in her early thirties and neatly dressed in a blouse and trousers. The cottage was small but immaculate, and it reminded me of a show home. It was bland and beige, the cushions were all plumped up and there wasn't a thing out of place. It couldn't have been more different from my house, which was full of pattern and colour, with knick-knacks on every surface. There were three cats curled up asleep on the sofa.

'Oh, don't mind them,' said Sharon. 'They're very tame.

'Would you like a cup of tea?' she asked.

I could tell she was on edge as she kept wringing her hands as she spoke.

'That would be lovely,' said Liz.

We sat in silence in the living room while Sharon made the tea. I noticed there were mirrored cabinets all the way along the living-room wall and they were full of china rabbits wearing different outfits and playing musical instruments and reading books.

'What lovely ornaments,' said Liz.

'They're Bunnykins by Royal Doulton,' Sharon said proudly. 'I've been collecting them for years.'

They were the kind of keepsakes that babies or children are given for their christening and they were very childlike. I found them a bit eerie. Somehow it felt like these little figurines were watching us. Even though there must have been close to a hundred of them, I could see there wasn't a speck of dust on any of them. Everything in that living room gleamed and sparkled, and the smell of Pledge mixed with a sickly sweet vanilla air freshener hung in the air. Either Sharon had cleaned and tidied especially for us or, as I suspected, this was how she always lived.

When she'd made the tea, Sharon sat down on the sofa next to Liz, while I was on an armchair.

'Thank you for agreeing to see us,' said Liz. 'As I explained on the phone, I'm your daughter's social worker and this is Maggie, the foster carer who Ruth has been living with for the past few months since she was taken into care.'

At the mention of the words 'taken into care', I could see Sharon's face crumble. She could hardly look at us.

'I thought Maggie could have a chat to you about Ruth and tell you anything you wanted to know,' Liz told her.

'When's the last time you saw her?' I asked her gently.

'Seven years ago,' she said, fiddling with the rings on her fingers. 'The day I left their dad Ian. Ruth was six and David was nine.'

She looked up at me.

'I know what you must be thinking,' she said in a quiet voice. 'You must think I'm terrible for leaving my kids like that. But I didn't leave them lightly. I wanted to take them with me but I had no choice.'

'We're not here to judge you,' I said. 'It doesn't matter what we think. I'm just here to tell you a bit about Ruth and what she's like.'

However, Sharon obviously felt the need to explain herself.

'I would never have left him if I'd known what he was going to do to her,' she said, her voice starting to crack with emotion.

'Why did you leave?' Liz asked gently.

'I couldn't take any more,' she sighed. 'I'd hit rock bottom in my marriage. Ian had beaten any self-esteem out of me, I didn't work and I had to beg for money for everything, even for things for the kids.

'He was very controlling and drank too much.

'When I found out he was having an affair with Marie I was shocked as she was my best friend, but it did give me an escape route. I knew he would never let me take the kids with me but I had to get out.

'I had nothing – no house, no job, no money. I couldn't take the kids with me and at least I knew if I wasn't around, Marie would look after them.'

Sharon's eyes filled with tears.

'I hoped in a few months, when I got sorted, then the children could come and live with me, but it took a lot longer than that for me to get back on my feet.

'Although Ian was terrible to me I never thought he'd lay a finger on one of his own children.'

She burst into tears.

'My poor little girl,' she sobbed. 'I thought she'd be safe with her dad. How could he do that to her?'

Liz reached out and put her arm on Sharon's shoulder and tried to comfort her but she was absolutely distraught.

'I feel so guilty,' she wept. 'It's all my fault. I'll never forgive myself for leaving her.'

'Sharon, you can't blame yourself' I said, passing her a tissue. 'You weren't to know what was going to happen.'

Suddenly, it was as if she was embarrassed that she'd broken down in front of us. She blew her nose, dabbed her eyes and did her best to compose herself.

'Have you had any contact with the children at all?' Liz asked.

'After a year or so I got in touch with Marie and said I'd like to see the kids,' she said, blowing her nose. 'Up until that point I was too afraid of Ian knowing where I was.

'Marie said she'd asked him but he'd said no as it would upset and confuse the kids. She said he wouldn't like it and that I knew how angry he got. I was still so frightened of him, so I just left it.

'Marie wrote to me the odd time and sent me a few photos of them, though.'

She paused.

'I wanted to see them,' she said. 'I never stopped thinking about them, you know. Wondering how they were getting on at school and if they ever thought about me.'

I could see she had so much guilt about leaving them.

'What about David?' she asked. 'How's he getting on? Is he OK at school?'

'I'm sorry, I can't help you there,' I said. 'I have seen him a few times but he doesn't actually live with me. He's with another foster carer.'

Sharon looked confused.

'Why aren't they living together?' she asked.

'We didn't place them together because we didn't think it was in their best interests,' Liz told her. 'They both had very different needs and we felt Ruth especially needed more one-to-one attention after what she'd experienced, and to support her through the police questioning and the court case.'

Sharon looked exhausted.

'Do you mind if I nip outside for a quick cigarette?' she asked.

'No, you go ahead,' said Liz. 'I can put the kettle on if you want?'

'Thank you,' she said.

While Sharon was smoking and Liz was making the tea, I nipped to the loo. As I walked through the living room I noticed two heart-shaped gold frames on a windowsill. There were two photos side by side in the hearts – one of a little girl and the other a young boy. When I saw the long dark hair and familiar blue eyes I knew instantly it was Ruth. She couldn't have been more than three in the photo and what struck me was her big smile.

She looks so happy, I thought sadly.

That must have been before her mum left and the abuse started. The other picture must have been David.

I eventually found the tiny downstairs toilet that was as pristine and immaculate as the rest of the house. There were two bowls of potpourri and I couldn't believe it when I saw the toilet paper had a corner turned down like I'd seen once in a posh hotel in London. I suspected that Sharon liked everything 'just so'. It was the polar opposite to how Ruth was and I'd already started to worry how Sharon would cope if she did want Ruth, her messy, careless daughter, to come and live with her. I knew it was more important than ever to give her the full picture about Ruth, and not rose-tint things, especially in relation to her personal hygiene. I could imagine Sharon's reaction to some of the things that had gone on in our house since Ruth had come to live with us. She didn't seem like the kind of person who would be able to deal with a parcel of poo in her airing cupboard.

'Your daughter's a very complex character and understandably she's got quite a few issues after everything that she's been through,' I said, after another cup of tea.

I told her about Ruth's anger, bitterness and insecurity.

'We've had quite a few problems around her hygiene and keeping herself clean, and she struggled to cope with starting her periods.'

I could see Sharon's eyes fill with tears again as I told her the reality about her daughter. It must have been so hard for her to hear.

'A lot of this is because of the abuse she suffered so hopefully after the court case and over time it will get better.

'School has also been tricky for Ruth.'

I explained how a residential school had been suggested at first because of the behavioural problems she'd had in the past but that I was dead against it.

'She used to love going to preschool when she was little,' said Sharon, smiling at the memory. 'She couldn't wait to get there on a morning and went running in with no problem whatsoever.'

'She's doing OK at her new school,' I said. 'Her behaviour's nothing like as bad as it was before and she's less disruptive. She seems to have settled in OK, although she struggles to make friends and she finds it hard academically.'

'The next few months are going to be particularly challenging for her as we approach the court case,' said Liz.

'Already I can tell that she's very nervous and anxious about it,' I said. 'I think the idea of being in the same court as her father and having to give evidence against him is understandably preying on her mind.'

'But we're going to be offering her a lot of support and care, and we're organising counselling for when all the legal proceedings are over,' added Liz.

I could see Sharon was taking it all in and I had the feeling that nothing we said could possibly put her off. She desperately wanted to see her daughter and nothing would change that.

'She just needs her mum around,' she said. 'Once she's got me then everything will be OK.'

Liz and I looked knowingly at each other. We both knew from experience that it certainly wasn't going to be as easy as that. Issues caused by years of trauma and abuse don't disappear overnight, plus we didn't know how Ruth, and also David for that matter, would react to the news that their biological mum wanted to see them again. They might be angry with her for abandoning them and Ruth might even blame her for the abuse. Sharon needed to be prepared for the fact that they might not welcome her with open arms.

'Have you got any questions that you want to ask Maggie?' Liz said.

'Has Ruth got lots of friends?' she asked.

'She struggled at first to make friends,' I said. 'But as time goes on I'm hoping that will change.'

'Does she like make-up?' asked Sharon. 'When I was her age I was really into that.'

'She's a bit young for make-up,' I said. 'Ruth's quite childlike in her behaviour and she's a bit of a tomboy. She likes playing with Lego and Duplo and constructing things and riding her bike.'

I looked at Liz and she nodded as she knew exactly what I was thinking.

'I've got some recent photos of her if you'd like to see them?' I asked.

Sharon's face lit up.

'Oh, yes,' she said. 'Yes, please, that would be wonderful. The only photos I've got of her and David are from donkey's years ago.'

I got the photos out of my bag. They weren't particularly good ones. Ruth wasn't fond of having her picture taken and in most of them she was scowling at the camera.

'That was taken the other weekend up on the hills near where I live,' I said. 'Ruth enjoys going up there and running around with the other kids.'

Sharon looked at it and her eyes filled with tears.

'She looks so grown up,' she sighed, a single tear snaking down her cheek. 'But I can still tell it's her. Her lovely dark hair's the same.'

She couldn't stop staring at it.

'And this one was taken at Pizza Hut on her birthday,' I said.

'Gosh, she's so small and thin,' she said. 'Is she eating properly?'

'She was underweight when she first came to live with me but she's eating well now and has put a bit on.'

I could see Sharon's joy and sadness at seeing her daughter etched on her face.

'You can keep these if you want,' I told her.

'Oh, can I?' she said, surprised. 'Thank you, Maggie. Thank you so, so much.'

I was glad that I could bring a small amount of joy into this desperately sad situation.

Before we left I needed to ask Sharon a question.

'As you've got parental responsibility for Ruth now I wondered if there was something you could do for me?' I said.

'Of course,' said Sharon.

'Ruth's been desperate to get her ears pierced for ages but I've always said no. Partly because I thought she was too young and also because I couldn't do it without parental permission.

'I haven't told her this yet but I wanted to do something nice for her after the court case was over and I wondered if you'd let me take her to get her ears pierced?'

'Oh, I don't mind at all,' said Sharon. 'She deserves a treat after having to go through all that.'

After an hour, it was time to leave.

'It's been lovely to meet you,' I said.

'You too,' she said. 'It's nice to meet the person who's looking after my daughter and hear all about her.'

'I'll be in touch next week to have another chat,' said Liz as we finished our goodbyes.

'Well, how do you think that went?' Liz asked as we drove off.

'It was OK,' I said. 'Mum seems nice but I think she's being naive. As far as those kids are concerned, she abandoned them. She's a stranger to them so it's not necessarily going to be the emotional reunion she's craving. There's been too much water under the bridge for them to run back into her arms like nothing's happened.'

'If she does decide she wants to get back in touch with them then we'll do plenty of work with her to prepare her for that,' said Liz.

Sharon was consumed by guilt for leaving them all those years ago and my heart went out to her. She had been very upset and tearful when she talked about the abuse. Understandably, that's the bit that had destroyed her the most.

I was pleased that I'd had the chance to meet her. If she and Ruth were eventually reunited, it would help that I had already met her and had some kind of relationship with her. I was hopeful that Sharon would want to be reunited with her children and I thought it would be good for Ruth to have her biological mum back in her life.

'Do you think there's a possibility Ruth and David might go back and live with her permanently?' I asked Liz.

'It's too early to say,' she said. 'However, you know as well as I do that wherever possible we try to keep kids with their biological families. If Mum's keen then we can start looking into it.'

A week later Liz rang me to say Sharon had been in touch.

'She's one hundred per cent sure that she wants to meet the kids again and ultimately she'd like them both to come and live with her,' she said. 'She'd like to see them as soon as possible but she understands why we want to wait until after the court case, so she's happy to trust our judgement on that.'

I was so pleased that Ruth had this chance to be reunited with her mum, and perhaps go and live with her. Although I wasn't sure how she was going to react to the news.

In the meantime, before we could think about any reunions and Ruth starting a new chapter, it was time to finish the old one. With the trial fast approaching, Ruth had to be prepared for going to court to give evidence against her father. And I was absolutely dreading it.

TEN

Preparations

As the weeks went by and winter turned to spring, the court case started to creep towards us. It was April and Ruth had been with us for six months now. My hopes about her father changing his plea to guilty to avoid a trial faded and I knew the inevitable was drawing closer. We were going to court and we had to start preparing Ruth for that.

A few weeks before the case was due to start, Liz brought a solicitor and a detective round to the house to meet Ruth. Seeing these two grey-haired men in suits sitting there in the living room immediately put her on edge and made her nervous.

'Don't be worried,' said Liz. 'They're just here to tell you a little bit about going to court and what will happen.'

Ruth was next to me on the settee and she gave me an anxious look. She stared down at her hands and started peeling bits of skin from around her nails.

'I'm Graham and I'm the solicitor who's in in charge of the case against your father,' one of them said. 'It won't be me asking you questions in court but I've instructed a barrister and given him all the evidence and all the things you told the police about your father.

'I know the barrister Charles very well. He's a nice man and he knows all about what you've been through and he believes everything that you said.

'It's his job to stand up in court and tell the jury and the judge what happened to you and why your dad should be punished for hurting you.

'Does that make sense?'

Ruth nodded and I gave her hand a reassuring squeeze.

'Will I have to go in the court?' she asked.

Graham shook his head.

'Nope. You won't be going in the courtroom and standing in the witness box like adults do when they give evidence.

'You're going to be sitting in a special room where there will be a little camera,' he explained. 'There will also be a TV in there so you can see which person in the court is asking you questions or talking to you.

'That will either be a judge or a barrister. There are two barristers who will be asking you questions – my barrister Charles and your father will have his own barrister.'

'Are they the people you see on the telly who wear those funny wigs?' asked Ruth.

'Yes, you're right,' said Graham. 'They normally do wear wigs but when they're talking to you they will probably take them off to make you feel more comfortable and at ease. Is that OK?'

Ruth nodded, although I think she was a little disappointed that they wouldn't look like they did on the TV. She was very quiet when all this was going on, although I could see her listening intently and taking it all in. As the solicitor was talking, she shifted up nearer and nearer to me on the sofa until she was practically sitting in my lap. I put my arm around her and she snuggled into me.

'Have you got any other questions that you want to ask Graham while he's here?' I said to her.

'Will I have to see my dad?' she said straight away.

I knew that this was her biggest fear.

'Don't worry, you won't be able to see him,' he said. 'You won't ever be in the same room as him.'

'Can Maggie be in the special room with me when they're asking me questions?'

The solicitor shook his head.

None of us could be in there, as we could then be accused of influencing what Ruth said.

'Maggie will be in the waiting room with you beforehand,' Liz told her. 'When it's time for you to give evidence, the court official will come and take you to the room, and Maggie will wait there.'

'Don't worry, I'll be there when you come out,' I said.

'But what if you need a wee and you're in the toilet when I come back?' Ruth asked.

'Then I'll make sure I go to the loo before you're called to give evidence.' I smiled. 'Don't worry, whatever happens or however long it takes, I will be there.'

The detective explained that they'd arranged for Ruth, Liz and I to visit the Crown court a couple of weeks before the trial to have a tour round.

'You'll be able to see all the places we've been talking to you about today,' the solicitor said. 'You can have a look around the courtroom itself and the room where the camera is, as well as the waiting room. Then you'll know exactly where you're going.'

'Is there anything else you want to ask?' asked Liz, but Ruth shook her head.

The poor girl looked terrified. I think talking about it had made it seem all the more real to her.

She went upstairs to play in her bedroom while the rest of us had a chat.

'That seemed to go OK,' said the solicitor.

'Thank you for being so gentle with her,' I told him. 'Understandably she's dreading giving evidence against her dad.'

'Have you got any questions?' he asked.

'Do you know yet when Ruth will have to give evidence?' I asked.

'We've got a preliminary date for the trial and I'd say it will probably last about two weeks at the most,' said the solicitor. 'At the minute we're expecting Ruth to be called up on the third day but we won't be able to let you know for sure until nearer the time.'

I'd already been up to Ruth's school and told them about the court case.

'I've had a chat to the head and explained what's going on and he's given Ruth the two weeks of the trail off anyway,' I said.

'We'll try, wherever possible, to get her evidence over and done with in one day so she doesn't have to come back to court,' the solicitor told us. 'But there is always the possibility she could be recalled later if the jury want to check anything.

'I know she's going to be nervous, that's only natural after everything she's been through. But hopefully once she's seen the court and knows exactly what will happen she'll be a bit more at ease with it all.'

'I hope so,' I said.

When the solicitor and the detective had gone, Liz stayed behind for a chat.

'How's Ruth doing?' she asked. 'Is she coping OK?'

'Well, you've seen her,' I said. 'She's like a different person.'

Over the past few weeks, the mouthy, stroppy young woman had been replaced by a scared, vulnerable little girl who needed constant reassurance.

'She's scared,' I said. 'She's worried about court and what's going to happen to her father.

'She's so clingy; it's like having a toddler. She wants to know where I am all the time and she gets anxious if she can't see me.'

'You're obviously giving her lots of support,' said Liz.

'I'm trying,' I said. 'I'm talking to her about it and giving her plenty of affection.'

Ruth had never been one for physical contact but now it was as if she craved it. She insisted that I did her hair for her every day before school and she wanted to be next to me all the time. Whenever I turned around, she was there. If we were watching TV in the living room she would pull my arm around her and snuggle under my armpit and she kept coming over to me for hugs.

'The plus side of all this is the game-playing has stopped,' I said.

It was true. The aggression and the attitude had gone and, for the first time, she was allowing us to see the real her – the traumatised little girl who I'd expected in the first place. Although

I hated the fact she had to go through this, it was nice to finally see her let down her barriers and be herself. She'd stopped picking on Lily, and she and Louisa were getting on better too. I hoped it was the last we'd seen of her tough girl act.

I tried to do practical things to help Ruth get ready for court. The day after the solicitor's visit, I took her shopping.

'Choose a soft toy,' I told her. 'And that can be your special cuddly who comes to court with you.'

I wanted her to have something physical she could hold that would bring her comfort while she was giving evidence. Ruth picked out a white fluffy cat wearing a red velvet collar with a bell on it.

'I'm going to call it Kit Cat,' she said.

'Even though I'm not allowed to come into the room with you when you give evidence, Kit Cat will,' I said. 'He'll look after you.'

For the next few weeks, Ruth slept with Kit Cat and took him everywhere with her and I was constantly giving him hugs and kisses.

Liz had warned us that there would be a lot of waiting around on the day so we bought some colouring books, word searches and some new pens to help pass the time. Although Lily was too young to understand what was going on, Louisa knew that Ruth had to go to court and she was very patient with her.

'These are for you,' she told her one day. 'I know you like them.'

She gave her one of her favourite pencil cases and some of her beloved smelly pens. I could tell that gesture meant the world to Ruth.

I also went shopping for an outfit for her to wear to court. I wanted her to look smart but I also felt it was important that she looked her age and that she looked like a child. I didn't take Ruth with me as I knew she'd want something more grown up. I went to Next and bought her a navy cord skirt and a white blouse with a Peter Pan collar. When I showed it to Ruth, she wasn't impressed.

'That's so babyish,' she moaned. 'I'm going to look stupid.'

'You need to look smart,' I told her. 'And I want you to look like you're twelve, not a teenager.'

The stress of the impending court case started to take its toll on Ruth. Old issues reared their heads again. I noticed that she'd started to smell and her hair was all greasy and I realised that she was skipping showers and probably not brushing her teeth either. I knew I had to take control before it escalated.

One night I went upstairs and handed her a towel.

'You need to have a shower before you go to bed because you didn't have one this morning,' I said.

'Yes, I did,' she replied.

'Ruth, you and I both know that you didn't and you didn't have one yesterday either, so please get in the shower.'

'OK,' she sighed.

Thankfully we were a lot more open about things now and it wasn't such a battle.

'I know you think I'm being mean,' I told her. 'And I know that you're really scared and worried about the court case but in the meantime everything else stays the same.

'That includes having a shower every day and brushing your teeth in the morning and at night and I'm going to keep nagging you until you do it.'

Ruth nodded. I wrapped my arms around her and gave her a hug.

'I know this is hard for you but don't take it out on yourself,' I said, kissing the top of her head. 'Remember it's not your fault. This is a man who was supposed to be looking after you but he didn't.'

I knew she was having trouble sleeping as well. At night I heard her tossing and turning and shouting out in her sleep. One evening I heard her get up to go to the toilet but when she went back to her room, her light didn't go off and I could hear the floorboards creaking. I couldn't get back to sleep so I decided to go and check on her.

'Ruth?' I called out quietly. 'Are you OK in there?'

I peeped around the side of her door. She was pacing up and down her bedroom in her pyjamas.

'What if people don't believe me, Maggie?' she said, her eyes wide with worry and fear. 'What if he gets off?'

'Of course people will believe you,' I said. 'Everyone believes you. It wouldn't have got to court otherwise.'

She didn't look convinced.

'You know when you were checked by a doctor before you came to live here? Well, she examined you and what she found backed up what you were saying.

'It's not just you saying it, there is lots of evidence about what your dad did to you.

'Everyone believes you and whatever else happens, you're safe and you'll never ever have to live with your dad again. He can't hurt you any more.'

Unfortunately, I couldn't reassure Ruth that he wouldn't get off. I just hoped that that wouldn't happen. I couldn't even think about the effect that him being found not guilty would have on Ruth. But I had a belief in the court system and I hoped that there was enough physical evidence for him to be convicted. He had to be, for Ruth's sake.

'Now you need to stop worrying and get back to sleep,' I said, leading her over to bed.

As I tucked her in, I noticed that her fingernails were all ragged, bitten and bleeding.

'What have you done?' I gasped.

'I was just picking at them,' she said.

'You need to get some sleep,' I said gently. 'You're going to be exhausted for school in the morning.'

Just over a week before the case was due to start, Ruth, Liz and I went to look around the Crown court. I hoped that seeing where she had to go would help take away some of Ruth's fear.

It was an old Victorian building and it was very grand and imposing.

'We'll go in the back way where you will come in on the day,' said Liz. 'So you don't have to go in the front entrance along with everybody else.'

Ruth seemed to be handling it OK and was quite curious and excited about being shown round. I could see that she was enjoying being the centre of attention and feeling important.

'Have you been here before?' she asked Liz.

'Yes, loads of times,' she said. 'I've been involved in lots of different cases.'

Graham the solicitor was there to meet us, along with a grey-haired woman in her fifties.

'Hello again, Ruth,' he said. 'I wanted to quickly introduce you to Hazel from Witness Care.

'She's going to look after you while you're at court and she'll be the one sitting with you in the room on the day when you're giving evidence.'

She was very smiley with a kind face.

'It's lovely to meet you, Ruth,' she said. 'I'm going to show you around the court and answer any questions you might have.'

'I'll leave you in Hazel's capable hands and we'll see you in a week or so,' Graham said.

He left and Hazel turned to us.

'Right then, let's start our grand tour. Have you ever been in a court before?'

Ruth shook her head.

'Well, the rooms you'll be seeing today might not be the exact ones that you'll be in on the day but they'll look the same.'

We followed Hazel down one echoey corridor after another. It was like a rabbit warren and Ruth kept looking behind her to check that I was still there.

'I'm going to take you to see one of the waiting areas first,' said Hazel.

It was a small room, very nondescript and bland. There was a table with a jug of water on it, a couple of office chairs, a box of toys and a few ragged children's books that had seen better days.

'This is the room that you'll be in with Maggie while you wait to be called to give evidence,' she said.

'How long will we have to sit in here?' asked Ruth, looking horrified.

'I'm afraid I can't tell you that,' she said. 'You'll have to come to court in the morning around nine thirty and then you could be called at any point after that.

'They'll try and get it over with as quickly as they can but you might want to bring some books or games with you to help pass the time in case you have a bit of a wait.'

Next she led us down some more corridors.

'Don't worry about remembering where to go because I'll take you,' she said. 'But when you get called to give evidence we'll go into a room like this one. It's all set up like it will be on the day.'

Ruth hesitated outside the door and for the first time that morning she looked anxious. I think the reality of what she was going to have to do had suddenly hit her.

'Come on, lovey,' I said, holding out my hand to her. 'Let's go in and have a look.'

She took my hand and I led her into the room. It was another bland, windowless space. There was a chair in the middle, a camera on a tripod in the corner and a desk with a screen to one side of it.

'Is that where I'll see everyone on the TV?' Ruth asked nervously.

'Yes, just the barristers and the judge and you'll talk into the camera,' said Hazel.

Next she took us to see a courtroom.

'You won't have to go in there at all on the day but I thought you might like to have a look round as you'll see it on the screen.'

We walked into the main entrance area and through to one of the courts.

It was huge and imposing with all the dark wood panelling and the huge gold crest on the wall behind the judge's bench.

'It probably seems very big and scary because it's empty but normally it's full of people.'

Ruth looked terrified as she stared at the dock. It was a wooden box with a glass-panelled screen around it.

'Is that where he will sit?' she asked.

'Yes,' said Hazel. 'Your dad will be safely behind that screen. Have a peep inside if you want.'

Ruth and I peered into the dock and saw there was a little staircase leading down from it.

'That will take your dad straight from the cells up to the court,' she said. 'So there's no way that you'll bump into him. He's brought in a different entrance to the court from everyone else and he's even got his own stairs.'

That seemed to reassure Ruth. Hazel pointed out where the judge and the jury would sit and also the two barristers.

'The camera will be positioned so you can see the judge and the barristers,' she said.

'So, what do you think?' she asked.

'It's very fancy and big,' said Ruth.

Afterwards, Hazel showed us where the toilets were and the canteen.

'The court normally has an hour's break for lunch so you can grab something to eat there,' she said.

'What if they don't have any sandwiches I like?' Ruth asked me. 'Do they sell crisps?'

'Yes, I'm sure they sell crisps.' Hazel smiled.

'I tell you what, we'll bring our own packed lunches with us on the day so then we know there will definitely be something that you like to eat,' I said.

We were done and dusted in just under an hour.

'What did you think?' asked Liz.

Ruth shrugged. I could tell she'd put her guard back up and was doing her nonchalant, not bothered face.

'It was alright,' she said. 'Bit boring.'

'Well, I thought it was really useful,' I said.

Afterwards, we went for a walk. There was a shopping centre nearby where I spotted a toyshop.

'Let's go and pick out a new game that we can bring to court with us,' I said.

I thought Ruth deserved a treat after going through that. She chose Junior Scrabble and we kept in in Liz's car so she could bring it to court for us on the day.

Ruth seemed fine with her visit to the court, but it had made it seem all the more real to me. It had brought it home that this was really happening and only in just over a week. All I could hope was that the jury would believe Ruth, and justice would be done. Because if it wasn't, then the fallout was going to be devastating.

ELEVEN

A Chance to Escape

With just over a week to go before the court case started, I had a brainwave.

I phoned Liz straight away.

'I've had what I think is a good idea, and I wanted to run it by you,' I said.

'Go on then,' she laughed. 'Am I going to like it?'

'I want to take Ruth away on holiday,' I told her. 'Me, her and the other kids. Somewhere by the sea, like Dorset or Norfolk.'

'What about the court case?' she asked.

'Well, if I get permission to take the kids out of school then we can go away for a week and still be back in time for Ruth to go to court and give evidence,' I said.

The more I thought about it, the more I knew it was the way to go. It would be the perfect distraction for Ruth and for all of us before she had to go to court. Being on holiday would hopefully take her mind off things and help her relax and catch up on sleep.

'As each day passes, she's getting more and more stressed,'

I explained. 'She's not sleeping, she's picking at her food. It's on her mind 24/7.

'She's weary now so by the time it actually comes to her going to court she's going to be exhausted, and I'm worried that she won't be able to cope. But I think if we went away it would give her a bit of peace and quiet, and a chance to recharge her batteries.'

'If you think it would help and you can assure me that you'll definitely be back in time for court then I'm happy to support it,' said Liz.

'Thank you so much,' I said.

When I get an idea like this into my head I am like a dog with a bone. I wouldn't let the holiday idea drop until it was sorted. I got straight on the phone to the children's various schools to explain the special circumstances and hopefully get permission to take them out of school for a week. Thankfully they were all very supportive. Then I rang a holiday letting company.

'I know it's short notice but I wondered if you'd got any seaside properties free next week?' I asked.

'I've got a cottage in Devon,' the man on the phone said. 'It's only small but it's in a pretty little fishing village and within walking distance of the beach.'

'It sounds like just the job,' I said.

I booked it for the following week so it meant we left in two days. It was perfect timing – we'd get back and then Ruth would be due in court the following day.

I knew that she desperately needed this time away. It would be a chance for her to get out of the routine, to be away from social workers, solicitors and police officers, and relax and be a child again. Now all I had to do was break the good news to her and the other girls. I couldn't wait to tell her and I was sure that she'd be delighted.

'I've got a bit of a surprise for you all,' I told Louisa, Lily and Ruth that night after we'd finished dinner. 'How do you fancy a last-minute holiday?'

'What do you mean?' asked Ruth, looking concerned.

'I thought we could all do with a bit of a break so I've booked a week in a cottage down in Devon,' I said. 'We leave in a couple of days.

'I thought it would be a lot quieter and nicer outside of the school holidays.'

I didn't want to single Ruth out and say we were going away now because of her and the court case. However, I don't think Louisa and Lily would have cared – they were ecstatic. They'd been to Devon with me before and loved it, and they were delighted about having time off school.

'I'm going to go up to my room and start packing now,' said Lily excitedly.

'Lily, we're not going for a couple of days so you've got plenty of time,' I laughed.

While the other two were jumping around the kitchen with joy, Ruth was quiet.

'What do you think?' I asked her. 'Are you pleased?'

'I'm just wondering what's going to happen to me,' she said sadly.

'What do you mean, what's going to happen to you?'

'I mean, where will I go when you lot are on holiday?'

'Don't be daft,' I told her. 'You're coming with us. We're all going.'

'I bet I'm not,' she said. 'You're moving me to another foster carer's, aren't you? You're just not telling me.'

I couldn't believe what I was hearing. My heart sank.

'Ruth, I would never do that,' I said. 'I thought we all deserved a holiday and the break would do us good.'

'You're lying,' she sighed. 'I know it. You're going to get me to pack my case and then make me go somewhere else.'

I was shocked that she thought I was cruel enough to do that to her.

'Do you want to come?' I asked her.

'Well, yeah, but I don't have much choice if you don't want me to, do I?' she said.

I couldn't win. No matter what I said or how much I tried to persuade her, Ruth refused to believe that she was coming with us. When I was tucking her in that night I tried one last time to reassure her again but she still wasn't having any of it. Those old wounds were proving desperately hard to heal.

The next day I talked about the holiday in the hope that she'd come to her senses.

'Lily, I need you to go and find your swimming costume and check that it still fits you and, Louisa and Ruth, I want you to do the same,' I said at breakfast.

'No point me checking my cossie because I ain't coming, am I?' sighed Ruth.

Louisa rolled her eyes. She and Lily were starting to get exasperated.

'Let's bloody well leave her behind if she's going to be like that,' she said. 'I don't know what's up with her.'

All I could think was that holidays were treats and in Ruth's eyes she didn't think that she deserved them so therefore she wasn't coming. In her mind, this was all one big, cruel trick.

Even the night before we were due to leave, Ruth still didn't believe it. While the rest of us were running round the house frantically packing our cases, she sat there watching.

'Look, Ruth, this is getting ridiculous,' I said. 'You need to start packing. We're leaving early tomorrow morning.'

But she refused point-blank.

'You want me to pack so you can move me to another foster carer's,' she said. 'I know what you're doing.'

'Ruth, why are you saying this?' I asked, half-exasperated, half-pleading.

'Because I just know,' she said.

'Well, you think what you like, but your case needs to be packed because it's got to go in the car with the rest of our stuff.'

I was so frustrated with her I marched into her bedroom and started chucking her clothes into a suitcase.

'If you won't do it, then I suppose I'll have to,' I said.

Ruth sat on the bed, glaring at me.

'Seven pairs of knickers,' I said in a sing-song voice. 'Four T-shirts, a swimming costume . . .'

'I told you I don't need a swimming costume,' said Ruth. 'I bet my new foster carers won't take me swimming.'

I tried not to get annoyed but it felt like I was banging my head against a brick wall. This was supposed to be a treat for her but when was she going to believe me? Maybe this hadn't been such a good idea after all?

The following morning was a flurry of activity as we got ready to leave. Ruth dragged her feet about everything – getting dressed, having a shower. I'd been trying to use up all the food before we went away so the cupboards were bare and Ruth had a hissy fit when there wasn't enough bread for her to have three slices of toast.

'You'll just have to have two, won't you, like you normally do?' I said, my patience running thin.

Ruth sat in the living room, watching curiously out of the window while the rest of us loaded our stuff into the car.

'Where are you taking that?' she asked suspiciously as she saw me walk past the door dragging her suitcase.

'I'm putting your case in the car with all the others because, in case you hadn't noticed, we're going on holiday in ten minutes.'

Even though she huffed and puffed about it, I managed to persuade her to get in the car. Even that was a relief as I was worried that I physically wouldn't be able to make her come along.

'When are you dropping me off then?' asked Ruth, five minutes into the journey.

We all moaned and rolled our eyes.

'We're not dropping you off because *we* are all going on holiday to Devon,' I said. 'And by "we" I mean all of us. You are part of this family so you're coming too, whether you like it or not.'

Thankfully that seemed to shut her up. That was until we'd been on the road for hours when a voice piped up from the back seat.

'So, I'm coming with you then?'

'Yes, Ruth!' I sighed. 'You've always been coming with us. We're nearly there, for God's sake.'

Surely she must believe me now, I thought.

'Well, I don't like the sea,' she moaned. 'It's too cold.'

We all laughed at her grumpiness and I could have cried with relief that the message had finally got through.

'If you don't like it you can always find another foster carer to look after you down here,' said Louisa.

'I'm joking,' she added, and Ruth actually cracked a smile.

At last the mood had lifted. She finally believed she was on holiday, and I could see the relief in her face. What sort of life must this poor kid have led that she thought inviting her to come on holiday with us was a cruel trick?

'We're going to have a great time, Ruth,' I told her. 'Just you wait and see.'

It was a beautiful night as we drove into the lovely little seaside town. The sun was setting, the sea was sparkling and the air was warm. Before we'd even got to our cottage, the girls insisted on going to the beach, so I parked up near the seafront. I sat on the rocks with Ruth while Lily and Louisa ran straight down to the water's edge. We watched them rip their shoes and socks off and run into the sea for a paddle. The tide was coming in and they whooped and laughed as they skipped around in the waves. Ruth looked completely wide-eyed with wonder and I could tell she was entranced by it all.

'Have you been to the seaside before?' I asked.

She shook her head.

'Have you ever been on holiday before?'

'Not that I can remember,' she said. 'I've seen the sea on telly, but I didn't think it would be so loud. I can't believe how noisy it is.'

She was so in awe of things that the rest of us took for granted, like going on holiday and playing on the beach.

'Why don't you go and have a paddle too?' I said.

She ran to join the others and soon all three of them were laughing and splashing in the water. Their clothes were soaking wet but I didn't mind.

I sat and watched them from the rocks, enjoying the warmth of the sun on my face. I gave a huge sigh of relief and, for the first time in ages, I felt myself relaxing. I hadn't realised what a drain the last few months since Ruth had come to live with us had been on me. After the fuss Ruth had caused, I'd questioned whether going away so close to the court case was the right thing to do but I was so glad that we'd come. We'd been here less than an hour but already solicitors, court cases and social workers felt like thousands of miles away.

After I managed to drag the three of them away from the beach, we went to find our cottage. It was a quaint little place with three tiny bedrooms. There was hardly enough room to swing a cat but the girls didn't care and they ran around excitedly exploring every room. There were bunk beds in one room so Louisa and Ruth agreed to share.

'Louisa said I can have the top bunk,' said Ruth, who was absolutely delighted about that.

'Thank you,' I mouthed to Louisa.

It was a small gesture but I could tell it meant so much to Ruth.

I'd brought a chicken casserole and dumplings from home with us for our dinner and there was bread and milk already in the fridge courtesy of the holiday company.

'Look, Ruth, you can have three slices of toast tomorrow,' I told her and she gave me a big grin.

I warmed up the casserole on the hob and we all tucked in and chatted happily. I always worried when I took away foster children who had never been on holiday before about how they'd cope with the change in routine and being away from familiarity. Sometimes it could leave them feeling anxious and stressed because it reminded them of when they were first taken into care, however Ruth seemed fine. It was a risk doing it right before the court case but I was convinced that it would do Ruth the world of good to get away from home and have a change of scene, and thankfully I'd been right. The first night was incredibly peaceful and she slept much better than she had been doing at home before we left. In fact, it was well after 9 a.m. before any of us woke up. It was another lovely sunny day so we ate breakfast in our pyjamas outside in the pretty paved courtyard. You could smell the saltiness of the sea in the air and hear the seagulls squawking.

'What shall we do today?' I asked them.

'Let's go to the shops and explore the town,' said Louisa.

'The beach!' shouted Lily and Ruth in unison.

'We can do both,' I said. 'Remember we've got the whole week.'

Already there was a change in Ruth. I could see her relaxing and she became more childlike. As walked into town to get some shopping, she reached out for my hand and skipped along next to me.

It was lovely to see her play so nicely with Lily. At the beach the two of them got stuck into making sandcastles. Louisa and I watched as they worked away for hours, building walls, decorating them with shells and digging trenches leading down to the sea. As the tide started to come in, Ruth squealed with joy as their moats began filling up with water, and she and Lily danced up and down on the sand.

'I don't mind Ruth when she's like this,' said Louisa.

She was becoming more accepting of Ruth and we all felt a lot softer towards her.

'It's nice to see her smiling and happy,' I replied.

It really was. I could see glimpses of the child that she would have been, if it hadn't been for the abuse and the neglect. What she would have become and hopefully what she still could.

The next few days couldn't have been better. In between trips to the beach, we explored local beauty spots, spent pocket money on old-fashioned sweets and tacky souvenirs and went to a country fair with Morris dancers and fairground rides. Ruth loved every single minute of it.

It did us all the world of good to get away from the routine of school and homework, tea at 5 p.m. and bath and bed. I loved the flexibility of being on holiday. We slept in so we didn't have breakfast until late, and lunches were lazy picnics on the sand. One night I realised it was 8 p.m. and we were still sitting on the beach.

'Is anyone hungry?' I asked. 'I'll go and get us some fish and chips for tea and we can eat them on the beach.'

Ruth looked really anxious about it.

'Are we allowed to do that, Maggie?' she asked. 'What if we get told off?'

It was so sad to see how easily the old anxieties came creeping back; she was so worried about doing something wrong and spoiling the holiday.

'Of course we're allowed to,' I said. 'We're on holiday. I'm the adult here and I've said it's fine to eat chips on the sand.'

With all the fresh air and long days out, as soon as we got back to the cottage, we all collapsed straight into bed and were out like lights.

*

It was nice to see Ruth having fun and enjoying being with us. She finally felt she was part of our family and she liked it. I could see how happy and relaxed she was by her body language – even the way she walked had changed. Instead of shuffling along with her head down, dragging her feet, she seemed lighter somehow. She skipped or bounced along, she was very chatty and there was lots of smiling and laughing. She and Lily would giggle at silly things and it was only when I heard her laugh that I realised what an unfamiliar sound it was and how little I'd heard it before. It was idyllic – we were in a beautiful place, the sun was shining and we were all getting on well. I even started to wonder whether I should sell up and buy a property there.

Don't be silly, Maggie, I told myself. *You're on holiday. This isn't real life.*

One afternoon, a couple of days before the end of the holiday, we were sitting on the beach. Lily and Louisa were in the sea, and Ruth and I were chatting.

'Have you had a good time?' I asked her.

She nodded and gave me a big smile.

'What was your favourite part of the week?' I asked.

'I liked having ice creams, coming to the beach, eating fish and chips . . . everything really. I love it here,' she sighed.

'Me too,' I told her.

It was good to see her so happy and enthusiastic.

'There was one thing I was wondering,' I said. 'Why were you so convinced that you weren't coming with us?'

'Because that's what my mum and dad did,' she said sadly.

She couldn't even look at me as she told me how the whole family had often gone on holiday without her.

'One year they went to Tunisia. Everybody else went – all my brothers – but they left me behind at home with one of my mum's friends because they said I was a pain.

'Another time they went away to a caravan in Wales but I wasn't allowed to go because I'd been bad.'

My heart went out to her. I was glad, however, that she felt able to share what had happened with me.

'Why didn't you tell me all this?' I said. 'I would have understood then why you were feeling so anxious and unsure about this holiday.'

'I was too ashamed,' she said.

It was no wonder that she had such low self-esteem. Not even her own family had wanted to spend time with her and she'd felt she wasn't good enough to go on holiday with them.

That night when we got back to the cottage I wrote down what she had said in my notes for Liz.

The best thing about the holiday was that we didn't mention the court case the entire time we were away. It was absolute bliss. That was until the night before we were due to leave.

'I don't want to go back,' I sighed as we were packing.

'Me neither,' said Ruth. 'I've got that court thing, haven't I?'

'Yes, you have, but try to put it to the back of your mind,' I told her. 'It's still a couple of days before you've got to think about that.'

Even though it was on her mind she seemed a lot more relaxed about it after the time away from home.

'There's no point worrying about it, is there, Maggie?' she said. 'It's going to happen anyway.'

I smiled. That was the kind of thing I said.

'You're right, flower,' I told her. 'There's no point worrying about what you can't change.

'We'll get through it.'

As we drove home the next day, my heart started to feel heavy with dread and I could tell by Ruth's face that she was feeling it too. My only consolation was that our holiday had done her the world of good. She was happy, relaxed and well rested, and I knew she was going to go to court in the best possible state. I wished we could have bottled the magic of Devon and taken it home with us. However, there was no putting off real life any more.

When we got home I saw the answerphone flashing. It was a message from Liz.

'I hope you all had a great holiday,' she said. 'Sorry to have to burst the bubble but the trial has started, and Ruth's due at court at nine tomorrow morning. I'll see you there.'

Devon and our carefree days on the beach suddenly seemed a million miles away.

TWELVE

Facing the Fear

As I pulled open the curtains, I gasped in surprise. It was absolutely pouring with rain – completely different from the warm sun we'd had the day before. In some way, though, I felt the torrential downpour reflected the mood in our house that morning – dark, stormy and filled with dread.

I could tell that Ruth was nervous because she got up quickly when I called her. Normally when I woke her up on a morning, there would be a lot of huffing, puffing and moaning. After a couple of reminders, she'd stagger downstairs in a daze, still half asleep. But today she leapt straight out of bed as if she'd been awake and waiting for me to call her.

It was obvious that she was on edge because she was jittery and couldn't keep still. While I waited for her bread to toast, I could see her feet jigging about under the table and she tapped her knife against the side of her plate, making a chinking sound that went right through me.

'Are you OK?' I asked her. 'How are you feeling?'

'Fine,' she snapped, not looking at me.

I knew she was far from fine.

While Ruth had her breakfast, I got the others organised. Lily was going to my friend Heidi's house as she was taking her to school and looking after her afterwards until we got back from court.

'I don't want to go to Heidi's tonight,' she moaned. 'Why can't I come home?'

'I told you, flower, I've got a meeting,' I said.

'I can come to the meeting. I'll be really quiet, I promise,' she begged.

'It's a very important meeting and you won't be allowed to come, I'm afraid,' I told her.

She was dragging her feet about everything and it was so frustrating as Ruth and I needed to be out of the door by eight. Louisa, bless her, took over. She convinced Lily of the benefit of going to Heidi's and packed her school bag. She knew what was going on and was being as helpful as possible.

'I hope it goes OK today,' she told Ruth before she left. 'Here, take these if you want. For good luck.'

She handed her a couple of her favourite bracelets.

'Thanks,' said Ruth, putting them on.

When I looked at Ruth, I realised that the ghost girl had returned. She was pale and drawn as if she hadn't slept and there was a blankness to her face that showed me she'd shut herself down.

Neither of us said much to each other. There wasn't a lot I could say to reassure her. She knew as well as I did that she was going to have to get through this and hopefully by the end of the day it would be all over. I didn't know what questions were going to be put to her or what was going to happen at court.

She went and got dressed and when she came back down, I was struck by how lovely she looked. The outfit was perfect and she looked like a little girl not a grown-up woman. However, I could tell by her face that Ruth didn't like it so I didn't dare make any comments and kept my mouth well and truly shut. I knew if I complimented her, she would have a strop and refuse to wear the outfit, and today of all days we didn't need any arguments.

I checked through the bag I'd packed the night before that was filled with all the stuff we were taking to court with us – there was a packed lunch and a book each, puzzles, drinks, snacks, pens, colouring books and word searches.

'We must remember to get the Scrabble from Liz's car before we go in,' I said.

I was going to drive us there and we'd arranged to meet Liz in the court car park. In the car Ruth hardly said a word and I didn't push her.

'You can choose the CD,' I told her. 'Put on anything you want.'

She was really into dance music, which I loathed, and even though my head was thumping as she turned up the volume and the bass boomed out so loud the speakers shook, I didn't say a word.

Liz was already waiting for us when we pulled up outside the court.

'Oh, Ruth, you look gorgeous,' she said when she saw her get out of the car.

Ruth scowled at her.

Thank God it's too late for her to get changed, I thought to myself.

'Don't forget your new game,' she said, handing her the Scrabble.

'I don't want the stupid game,' she said to me. 'Here, you put it in your car.'

I knew she wasn't really angry about the game. This was her way of showing her distress about what she was about to do. Determined to keep the peace, I took the Scrabble back to my car and put it in the boot.

Liz explained that she wasn't allowed to come into our waiting room with us as she was due to give evidence before Ruth. She had to wait in another room until it was her turn to take the stand.

'I'll try to catch up with you later in the day when I've finished giving my evidence, but if I'm not able to then I'll ring you tonight, Maggie,' she said.

'You'll be fine, Ruth,' she said. 'Answer the questions honestly and tell the truth like you always have done.

'Would you like a hug?'

'No thanks,' she said.

We walked towards the back entrance where we'd gone when we had our tour. But just before we got to the security door, Ruth stopped dead in her tracks.

'Do you think he's here yet?' she said in a small voice. 'Am I going to see him, Maggie?'

'No, we're not going to see your dad,' I told her. 'This is a special entrance just for witnesses. Remember the staircase we saw underneath the dock? He'll be brought into court a completely different way so there's no chance of us bumping into him, and he'll have security guards with him.

'Try not to worry,' I said.

When I grabbed her hand I realised she was trembling with fear.

'Come on, we need to go in now,' I said.

'No,' she snapped. 'I want the Scrabble. Can you go and get it from your car?'

'Ruth, we've got to go in now,' I said. 'We haven't got time and you said you didn't want it.'

'Please, Maggie,' she said.

Normally I would have told her no way, but I bit my tongue and went and got the game for her.

Finally we were ready to go in. I pressed the intercom and someone buzzed us in. When we walked through, Hazel from Witness Care was waiting for us.

'Hello, Ruth,' she said. 'How are you holding up?'

'OK, I suppose,' she grunted.

'I'm still not sure what time you're going to be called up,' she said. 'Hopefully it will be today, but if it gets to two o'clock then they may decide to leave it until tomorrow.'

I knew the prosecution was keen for Ruth to get her evidence over and done with in one day so it didn't drag on for her.

Hazel took us through to the small windowless room where we'd have to wait. It was as bland and as characterless as the one we'd been shown on our tour round the court. She stayed in there with us and, in a way, it was helpful as it meant Ruth and I didn't talk about the case or anything connected to it. I was glad about that. I was deliberately avoiding talking about it with her as I didn't want to be accused of putting words into her mouth before she gave her evidence.

Hazel did her best to put Ruth at ease. They did a couple of word searches together and we all had a game of Scrabble. She walked her to the kitchen area to get her a drink and a biscuit, and she took her to the loo a couple of times. As the time passed, Ruth was getting more and more fidgety.

By 11.30 a.m. we were all getting restless.

'Do you have any more idea about when Ruth might be called?' I asked Hazel.

'Let me go and have a chat to the court clerk,' she said.

She disappeared off.

'I'm so bored,' yawned Ruth.

'I know, lovey,' I said. 'You're doing really well.'

I was fed up with that windowless pit too. I'd even resorted to reading the posters on the wall.

Clunk click every trip . . . Don't drink and drive . . . If you need to talk to someone in confidence about domestic violence . . .

Ruth and I both jumped when Hazel came back into the room.

'Is it time?' asked Ruth anxiously.

'Unfortunately, it's not going to be this morning,' she said. 'The court are going to break for an hour's lunch from twelve, so why don't you go for some fresh air and a bite to eat and I'll see you back in here at one?'

'OK,' I said.

I could see Ruth was relieved but also a bit annoyed that there was going to be more waiting around.

'Come on,' I said. 'Let's go for walk. We can eat our packed lunches outside.'

I knew Ruth was nervous about hanging around the court grounds. Even though I explained there was no way that her dad would be allowed to wander around outside and he'd be taken back to the cells, she still didn't believe it.

'What if we see my mum?' she said. 'Or my brothers?'

'I'll check with Liz, but I don't think any of them have been at court,' I said. 'And even if we did see them, you're with me, they can't hurt you and you don't have to talk to them if you don't want to.'

She didn't look convinced, so we walked to the nearby shopping centre and ate our sandwiches on a bench in the car park. As we were tucking in I noticed there was a Claire's Accessories there. It was one of Ruth's favourite shops so I thought I'd take her in and buy her a little treat.

'Do you fancy a wander round Claire's?' I asked when we'd finished our lunch. 'You can choose some slides or a new hairband if you like.'

'Yeah,' said Ruth. It was the first time I'd seen her smile all day.

Ruth was always indecisive and so she spent ages looking at all the hair things, then she decided she'd prefer to get some jewellery instead. I lost track of time and it wasn't until we were in the queue to pay for the hair bobbles she'd chosen that I looked at my watch.

'Oh my God, Ruth, it's five to one,' I gasped.

We were due back in court in five minutes. I was in a complete panic.

'I might get into trouble with the judge if they call you and you're not there,' I said.

We quickly paid and ran out of the centre and back towards the court as fast as we could. I was sweating and gasping for breath by the time we dashed around the back of the court and through our entrance. It was ten past one by the time we got back into the waiting room.

'I'm so sorry. We're here,' I panted, collapsing onto a chair.

'Thank goodness for that,' said Hazel. 'I was getting worried you weren't coming back.'

'Sorry,' I said. 'We got a little waylaid in Claire's Accessories, didn't we, Ruth?'

Ruth gave a sheepish smile.

'You've not missed much,' said Hazel. 'Court's resumed but I've not heard anything yet.'

So it was back to some colouring and another round of tea and biscuits. Just before 2 p.m. there was a knock on the door and a man poked his head around it. Hazel got up and went outside to chat to him. Ruth and I looked at each other nervously. Was this it?

'Liz is finishing off giving her evidence so they're probably going to be ready for you in fifteen minutes,' she said when she came back in.

Ruth looked pale and anxious.

'Don't worry,' I told her. 'You can do this. I'll stay here and wait for you, I'm not going anywhere and when you come out you'll come straight back to me.

'And remember, if it all gets too much then say that you need a break and they'll give you one.'

'Maggie's right,' said Hazel. 'You can have ten breaks if you need them. Everybody will understand.'

I picked up Kit Cat, Ruth's stuffed toy, and covered it with kisses.

'If you need a kiss or a cuddle from me when they're asking you questions then you've got Kit Cat,' I said, handing it to her.

Suddenly the door opened and the same man stuck his head in and nodded to Hazel. We both knew it was time.

'Right then, Ruth,' she said. 'Come on, let's go and get this over and done with.'

We stood up and I gave her a cuddle and a kiss. As I put my arms around her I could feel her frail little body shaking with fear.

She was terrified and her face was ashen. She looked so young and vulnerable, standing there clutching her cuddly toy. In a strange way, I was glad, as that was what the jury would see.

'Remember I'll be here waiting for you,' I said.

She gave me a weak smile before she disappeared out of the door.

To say that the next few hours dragged was an understatement. I sat in that room on my own, my head whirling with thoughts.

How was Ruth doing? What were they asking her? I hoped she felt able to ask for a break or a drink of water if she wanted one.

Please, please let it be OK.

I tried to read my book but I couldn't concentrate. I paced up and down, read the posters on the wall for the millionth time and bit my nails down to stubs.

After a couple of hours I was desperate for the toilet but I didn't dare go anywhere in case Ruth came back. Finally, nearly three hours after she'd left, the door swung open and Hazel and Ruth walked back in. Ruth looked absolutely exhausted and I could tell that she'd been crying as her eyes were all puffy and red.

'How are you?' I asked. 'How did it go?'

She didn't say a word. Instead she collapsed into my arms. I could tell she wanted to be held.

'She did really well,' said Hazel. 'She only had one break when she got a bit upset.'

'I'm so, so proud of you,' I whispered, kissing the top of her head that was still buried in my neck.

'Do you think they'll need her again?' I asked Hazel.

'I think they got everything they needed today so it's highly unlikely she'll be required again. However, it's always best to keep the days clear just in case.'

'Ruth's got the next couple of weeks off school so we're around if she needs to be recalled.'

'Fingers crossed, she won't be,' said Hazel.

After a hug, Ruth seemed a bit brighter and we packed up our things. Neither of us could wait to leave that room and I could tell Ruth was desperate to get away from the court as soon as possible.

On the way out, Hazel took me to one side.

'Liz said sorry that she didn't catch you but to tell you that she'll come round later tonight for a chat.'

'OK, great. Thanks for passing that on,' I said.

We were both glad to leave the court. The dark clouds had gone and we emerged into the car park to a sunny spring evening, blinking in the bright sunlight.

In the car Ruth was very quiet. I didn't push her to tell me anything as I could tell she was exhausted and emotionally drained.

Around half an hour into the journey she started to chat.

'The solicitor was right about them wigs,' she said.

'What do you mean?' I asked.

'The lawyer men had their wigs on when they started asking me questions and the judge got cross with them and told them to take 'em off.'

'You don't want to mess with a judge.' I smiled. 'What was he like?'

'It was a lady,' she said. 'I liked her. She was nice. She explained lots of things to me and told me to ask if there was something that I didn't understand.'

'Good. I'm glad she looked after you.'

After that she told me a bit more about the court – how she could see the judge and the two barristers on the TV screen.

'One man was really nice but the other one was horrible. He kept saying that I was making stuff up, but I wasn't.'

'Did you tell him that?' I asked.

Ruth nodded.

'I started off talking in a little voice but then I got all angry and told him that he was annoying me.'

I laughed. I could just imagine it.

'Good for you,' I said.

'Did you see your dad on the screen?'

Ruth shook her head.

'Do you think he could see me?' she asked.

I suspected that he would have been able to see her but I didn't want to say that to Ruth until I was sure so I said that I'd check with Liz.

It had been a long day. By the time we'd gone to Heidi's to pick up Lily and had a quick tea, we were shattered. I could see Ruth was relieved to be home.

'I don't want to talk about it any more,' she told me as we got out of the car. 'I want everything to be normal.'

She played a board game with Lily and then curled up in front of the telly. By 9 p.m. she was ready for bed.

'Maggie, please will you tuck me in?' she asked.

'Of course I will,' I said.

She obviously needed that comfort.

'I'm so proud of you,' I told her again as I pulled the duvet up around her and gave her a kiss on the head.

'Night night, sleep tight,' I said. 'Don't let the bed bugs bite.'

'If they do then squeeze them tight,' she replied.

She'd obviously heard me say the same rhyme to Lily every night.

I deliberately left her door slightly ajar and the landing light on so that if she woke up, she'd know instantly where she was and wouldn't be frightened. She'd been through so much today I was worried that she wouldn't be able to sleep or would have a restless night. However, she was so exhausted she nodded off straight away.

She'd been in bed about half an hour when Liz arrived.

'How is she?' she asked.

'Totally shattered but relieved that it's all over,' I said. 'She's fast asleep.'

Liz explained that after she'd given evidence she went back into the court to watch Ruth.

'She did so, so well,' she said. 'She was absolutely brilliant.'

She described how it had been funny when Ruth had got cross at the barrister for questioning her story.

'So, do you think they believed her?' I asked.

'Maggie, if you'd have heard it all, you'd have believed her.

'There was such a level of detail that you knew she couldn't be making it up. Horrendous things that a child that age wouldn't, or shouldn't know.

'That man put her through hell.'

I hadn't asked any details about the abuse up until now because I was so conscious about the court case but Liz and I were finally free to talk about it.

'She couldn't remember a time when it didn't happen,' she said, shaking her head. 'It's been going on since she was little.'

She described how Ruth had told the court that her stepmum would work three evenings a week, cleaning offices, and that's when the abuse would take place.

'Dad would tell her it was a special treat,' she said. 'She was allowed to stay up late and watch TV with him but the others weren't.

'Then he'd rape and abuse her.'

Horrific.

'He told her never to tell anyone about what happened otherwise terrible things would happen to her. She'd already been subject to quite a few nasty beatings at his hands so, of course, she believed him.

'Maggie, she honestly believed that he would kill her. The poor child must have been terrified.'

The reality was as awful as I had imagined and all at the hands of a man who was supposed to have loved and protected her. I hoped they locked him up and threw away the key.

'What about Mum?' I asked. 'Have you heard much from her recently?'

Liz nodded. She told me how Sharon had been ringing every day to see how the court case was going.

'She's been calling me most weeks since we met her to see how Ruth is doing and how she's coping. She's incredibly nervous about the court case too. She wants to be able to support Ruth but she understands why she's got to wait.'

'So she's still keen to see them?' I replied.

'Oh yes,' said Liz. 'She wants to meet her and David more than ever.

'I've told her that after the verdict, we'll put a plan in place.'

The verdict. That was the next hurdle to overcome.

'When do you think that's likely to be?' I asked.

Liz shrugged.

'Your guess is as good as mine. The barristers said the jury will hopefully go out some time next week.'

'Then it will finally be over and Ruth can start to move on,' I said.

I couldn't wait for that day and for Ruth to be able to take steps towards the future. A better, happier one, hopefully with her mum if that was what she eventually decided.

However, nothing was certain. I desperately hoped that Ruth's father would be found guilty and punished for the terrible things that he'd done to her. He had to be.

I knew that if he was found not guilty and walked free, it could destroy her.

THIRTEEN

The Verdict

The day after giving evidence, Ruth slept and slept. She finally came downstairs just after 11 a.m. I could see she was still incredibly tired but totally and utterly relieved.

'How are you feeling today?' I asked her.

'Glad that I've got it over with,' she said.

I knew her big fear was having to talk about the abuse in front of other people but she'd done it. However, one fear was replaced by another and now her new worry was that she was going to be recalled and would have to go back to court. Every time the phone rang, she jumped and looked at me, her eyes wide with concern.

'I don't wanna go back there,' she said. 'I don't wanna have to talk about it all over again.'

'I honestly don't think that will happen,' I said, trying my best to reassure her.

But we both knew there were no guarantees.

Liz was going to court every day, and every evening she'd promised to ring me with an update. As part of the defence's case, I knew Ruth's dad was due to give evidence the day after her and I was curious to know how he'd come across.

'What was he like?' I asked Liz when she rang that night.

'As you'd expect, a nasty piece of work,' she said.

She explained that he was still insisting that nothing had happened and he hadn't touched Ruth.

'What did he say about the physical evidence?' I said. 'Surely he can't dispute the injuries the police doctor found on Ruth?'

'Exactly,' said Liz. 'That's when he got very hassled. By the time the CPS barrister had finished with him he was a gibbering wreck.'

'Good,' I said.

I was glad to hear that the prosecution had ripped his defence apart. I only wished that I had been there to see it.

'The jury have got to believe it,' I said. 'You can't dispute medical evidence.'

'You can never be sure,' said Liz. 'You'd hope so but you never know what they're thinking.'

'Was there anyone there to support him?' I asked.

'No one,' said Liz. 'No sign of Ruth's stepmum. No other family. The public gallery was completely empty.

'I gather that Marie was called to give evidence earlier in the trial, but there's been no sign of her since.'

Although Ruth was relieved to have finished giving her evidence I could see that it had opened up a whole can of worms for her. After she'd given her initial police interviews, she'd spent the last few months blocking it out and not talking about it to anyone because she'd been told that she wasn't allowed to. But going through it again in court in such great detail had brought everything back. The plaster had been ripped off to reveal a red raw, gaping wound and her fear was very real again.

She started to worry about the verdict too. The next morning I looked over at Ruth while she was having breakfast and I could see something was wrong. The colour had drained from her face and her skin was almost translucent. It was as if I could physically see her fear.

'Are you thinking about your dad?' I asked.

She nodded.

'What if he gets off, Maggie, and I have to go and live with him again?' she asked.

'Whatever happens in court, I can assure you one hundred per cent that will never, ever happen,' I told her. 'What your dad did to you was wrong and you'll never have to live with him again or see him, if you don't want to.'

That night I heard her calling out in her sleep. When I ran in, she was sat bolt upright in bed, as white as a sheet.

'He was here,' she mumbled. 'He was right here in front of me.'

I knew exactly who she was talking about.

'He's not here, lovey. He's locked up in prison,' I told her. 'You're safe now.'

She was shaking like a leaf and all I could do was cuddle her.

'He will never be able to hurt you again,' I whispered as she whimpered in my arms. 'No one will ever allow it.'

Ruth became obsessed by the idea that her dad would turn up at our house.

'What would we do if he came here?' she asked.

'He won't,' I said. 'You're safe. Your dad doesn't know where you're living now, nor does any other member of your family for that matter.'

'What about David?' she asked. 'What if he tells them?'

'He's at his foster carer's and he's not in touch with them either. Besides, your dad is locked up in prison Ruth. He'd have to break out of there to get here and the guards wouldn't let that happen.'

But she was obsessed with going over it again and again, talking about what we would do. I went along with it in the hope that it would reassure her.

'What would happen if he turned up at the door?' she said.

'I would yell at him to get off my doorstep and I'd slam the door in his face and call the police, and they would come and arrest him and take him back to prison,' I said.

'But what if he burst in and you didn't have chance to slam the door?'

'I'd shout to you and you could run upstairs and hide in your bedroom, then I'd phone the police.'

Louisa was there while we were having this conversation and even she joined in to help reassure her.

'Yeah, while Maggie distracted him I'd go and ring the police so he couldn't hurt you,' she said.

'But what if the phone wasn't working?' asked Ruth. 'What would we do then?'

'Then one of us would go out the back door and run round to the neighbour's house and use their phone,' I told her.

No matter how ridiculous it seemed, her fear was real and I knew it was important for me to talk her through every scenario.

'What if he comes to the door and strangles you before you can warn me or call for help?'

'I'm not a small woman, am I?' I said. 'I'm tall and I'm strong and if he tried to strangle me on my doorstep I'd kick up such a fuss I'm sure someone would notice.

'I promise you, Ruth, I'll protect you.'

Even after all this time her dad still had power over her.

Ruth didn't seem interested in what was happening at court, instead she craved normality. She wanted everything to stay exactly as it had been in the house. I'd arranged for her to have two weeks off school around the trial and I felt she still needed that time to give her some breathing space. She needed the safety and security of routine and she was anxious about it. There was lots of checking that things were going to happen at certain times.

'We are having dinner at five like normal, aren't we?' she would ask.

I tried to help and wherever possible I stuck to mealtimes with military precision.

Ruth was terribly messy and one of her bad habits was getting lots of her crafting kits out in the kitchen and starting a new one without clearing the old ones away. One afternoon she was making some bracelets. When I walked in the kitchen later on I saw she'd got a chocolate coin-making kit out but there were still bracelets and beads strewn all over the place. Normally I would have pulled her up on it and made her tidy them away but I decided, just this once, to let it go.

I didn't want to come down hard on her so soon after the court case. She didn't deserve a hard time after everything she'd been through.

However, that evening Ruth marched into the living room looking upset.

'You're not being yourself, Maggie, and I don't like it,' she said.

'What do you mean?' I asked.

'I got the beads out and I didn't tidy them up and then I got the chocolate coins out too but you didn't say anything about the mess or tell me off.'

'Did you do that?' I asked. 'Did you make a mess?'

Ruth nodded.

'Well then, I'll tell you off now, shall I? Go and tidy them up, young lady.'

We looked at each other and burst out laughing. At least we could see the funny side but I knew Ruth was right. She was telling me she didn't want an easy ride or to be treated differently because of the court case and I had done exactly that. She wanted normality and stability, not sympathy, and I knew I'd done her a disservice.

'I'm sorry I was too soft on you,' I said. 'I promise I'll be my normal shouty self from now on.'

As the days passed, I kept things very quiet. We went up to the hills as I knew Ruth loved it and she seemed to be at peace there. We'd pick Lily up from school and go up there for a walk or spend the day at home. One afternoon I told her that I'd got a surprise for her.

'As a special treat I'm taking you into town to get your ears pierced,' I said.

Ruth's face lit up. She'd been begging to get them done for months and now Sharon had given me permission.

'I thought you deserved it after everything you've been through with the court case,' I said.

She was so excited, she even grinned through the pain as the woman in the department store pierced both her lobes. She absolutely loved the little sparkly studs that she'd chosen.

Three days after Ruth had given evidence, my phone rang mid-afternoon. My heart leapt when I saw Liz's number.

'What's happened?' I asked. 'Do they want Ruth to come back?'

'No, nothing like that,' she said. 'I'm ringing to tell you that the jury's gone out.'

'Already?' I gasped.

We'd been told the trial was expected to last two weeks but it had only been just over a week.

'Is that a good or a bad thing?'

'Good, I think,' said Liz. 'The CPS seems really pleased with the way it's going.

'They're unlikely to come back today so I'll pop round on my way home from court and let Ruth know.'

'Of course,' I said.

A couple of hours later Liz arrived and we sat Ruth down. We both knew there was no point using complicated legal language as she wouldn't understand it, so we tried to explain it in basic terms. We told her about the group of people who sat on the bench in court.

'They've been listening to what everyone has been saying and they heard your evidence,' said Liz. 'Now they go off into a room and they talk about it and then they'll make a decision.'

'About what?' asked Ruth.

'About whether they think your dad is guilty or not,' I said.

'But what if none of those people believe me?' she asked. 'What if they decide he didn't do it and he gets out of prison?'

'Ruth, none of us know what's going to happen but if he does get off then we'll deal with it then,' said Liz.

'The people that matter believe you, like me and Liz, the barristers and the police,' I told her.

I didn't even dare think about the consequences of Ruth's dad being found not guilty. The fallout would be unbearable. I couldn't help but think of the poor lad called Darryl that I'd fostered years ago. He'd been abused by a family friend and it had gone to trial. But the family friend was found not guilty, and Darryl was never the same again. After he'd left me he'd spiralled into depression, and had tried to kill himself several times. The last I'd heard was that he was living in a psychiatric home. He could never get over the fact that the jury hadn't believed him and that his abuser had walked free.

Please, God, don't let that happen to Ruth, I thought.

I wasn't sure how she'd react to the news that the jury had gone out, but she seemed pleased.

'At least that means I don't have to go back there again,' she said.

There was never any question about Ruth going to court to hear the verdict. It wouldn't be appropriate for a child of her age, and I knew there was no way she would want to see her dad.

'When those people come back and say whether they think my dad's done it or not, I want you to be there,' Ruth told me. 'I want you to be in court so you can tell me what they decide.'

'I'm happy to do that,' I said. 'But I'll have to check with Liz first because that's normally the social worker's job.'

I rang Liz the following morning – the jury's first full day of deliberations.

'If Ruth specifically wants you to be there for the verdict then that's fine,' she said. 'The CPS don't think the jury is likely to come back today but you'd better come to court tomorrow.'

The next day I arranged to drop Lily and Ruth at Heidi's. I left my car at her house and Liz came to pick me up.

It was the second day of deliberations and I knew all we could do was play the waiting game. We drank endless cups of tea and ate far too much vending-machine chocolate. It did, however, give me and Liz a chance to chat about what would happen after the court case.

'I'm trying to get some counselling organised for Ruth,' she said. 'I thought we'd start off with one session a week with a child psychologist for three months and see how it goes.'

'I think she needs it,' I said. 'When will it start?'

'Not right away,' said Liz. 'Whatever happens, I think she needs a bit of time after the court case to try and get her head together.'

As it approached three o'clock we were expecting to be told the jury was going to be discharged for the day and that we'd have to come back tomorrow. But then there was an announcement over the tannoy. All parties in our case had to return to the court.

'The jury must have come back,' said Liz, standing up and grabbing her handbag.

As we dashed to the public gallery, my heart was thumping. This was it. This was what we'd been waiting for. I felt sick with nerves and I was suddenly desperate for the loo, but the jury was filing in and there was no time to go anywhere. As they sat down in the bench, one of the jurors – an older lady – caught my eye and smiled.

'I think it's going to be OK,' I whispered to Liz.

'How do you know?' she asked.

'One of the women on the jury smiled at me.'

'She's probably just being friendly,' said Liz, who clearly thought I was mad.

Before the judge came into court, it was time to bring up the defendant. The dock was to one side of us and to get a proper view of Ruth's dad I had to twist my neck and swivel round in my seat. I didn't want to draw attention to myself, or for him to see me – I don't know why, because he didn't know me from Adam – but I had a quick look as I wanted to see him for myself. I wanted to see the sick, twisted man who had done this to Ruth.

Her dad looked exactly as I'd pictured him – a short, burly, aggressive-looking bloke with short, dark, curly hair. He was wearing scruffy grey joggers and a stained grey sweatshirt.

I thought of frail, petite Ruth being overpowered by this brute and I felt sick. He glared at the judge as she came into court.

'What verdict have you reached?' the judge asked the foreman of the jury.

As the foreman stood up and looked down at the piece of paper in his hands, I closed my eyes. I could feel my heart thumping out of my chest.

Please, please make the right decision. For Ruth's sake. Please believe her.

'Guilty of all charges.'

'Yes!' I gasped at exactly the same moment as Liz.

I hadn't meant to call out but I couldn't stop myself. Liz and I turned to each other and I gave her a hug. I was still in shock as the judge talked about Ian being kept on remand while pre-sentencing reports were prepared.

'You're due back in court for sentencing in four weeks,' she said. 'Crimes of this nature can only warrant a custodial sentence.'

As he was led out of the dock and down the stairs I could hear him shouting.

'I ain't done nothing wrong. She's a lying little bitch.'

I was so relieved and pleased that I could go home and tell Ruth that a court full of strangers had believed that she was telling the truth. No matter how compelling the evidence, you could never be sure what a jury was going to decide.

I rang Heidi from the pay phone at court.

'How did it go?' she asked quietly.

'Guilty of all charges,' I said.

'Oh, thank goodness,' she sighed. 'I was so worried. I've been on tenterhooks here.'

We decided that when Liz and I arrived, Heidi would take Lily and the other kids into another room so we could break the news to Ruth.

'Do you mind if I tell her?' I asked Liz.

Normally it would be the social worker's job to pass on significant news like that.

'Not at all,' she said. 'I know Ruth was keen to hear it from you.'

When we got to Heidi's, everyone was in the front room and the kids were playing. Ruth looked at us expectantly.

'Come on, Lily, do you want to bring the others and come and help me with something in the kitchen?' said Heidi.

Liz and I sat down on the sofa with Ruth.

'So what happened?' she asked.

'The jury found your dad guilty,' I said. 'And do you know what that means, Ruth? That means that they believed everything you said. The jury believed you and the judge believed you and now everyone knows that your dad did something very wrong and he's going to be punished.'

'They really believed me?' asked Ruth, a shocked expression on her face.

'Absolutely,' I told her, grabbing her hand and giving it a squeeze. 'They believed every word you said.'

She grinned as the news slowly started to sink in.

'Your dad's been sent back to prison for four weeks and then he's got to go back in front of the judge and she'll decide how long he's going to prison for.

'And she's already warned him that he will be going to prison for what he did to you.'

'I can't believe it, Maggie,' she said. 'I can't believe they really believed me.'

'Well, we can,' said Liz.

'What would you like to do now?' I asked her. 'Do you want to go out and celebrate?'

'I want to see David,' she said. 'I want to see my brother.'

Although she hadn't seen him for months, it didn't surprise me that she wanted to be with the only biological relative she still had in her life. Liz had already phoned his foster carer from court and told her about the guilty verdict, and she'd checked to see if he was free that night.

'How about we go and pick David up from his foster carer's and I can take you both out for tea?' asked Liz.

Ruth nodded.

I also think Ruth suspected that David still didn't accept that their dad had abused her and she wanted to prove to him that it was true. A courtroom full of people believed her, so now he had to as well.

Liz took Ruth off to pick up David while I drove Lily home. It was only when I got back and sat down that I realised I had a terrible headache. The day had been awfully stressful and I'd been hoping hard for that guilty verdict. If Ruth's dad had got off she would have been devastated and I didn't know how she would have coped.

When Ruth got back at seven she was still all smiles.

'Did you see David?' I asked.

'Yep,' she said. 'He knows what's happened to Dad, and he said he believes me.'

'Good,' I said. 'And so he should.'

I had a quick chat with Liz before she left.

'How did it go with David?' I asked.

Liz explained they had been quite cool with each other.

'They're not what I'd call close,' she said.

She explained that David hadn't been getting on with his current foster carer so he was being moved.

'No matter what he says, I think there's still a part of him that thinks Ruth is lying about the abuse,' she said. 'Also, he blames her for him being shunted around. He says he was alright with his dad and his stepmum, and he resents Ruth for them being taken into care.'

'It's tricky,' I said.

They might have been brother and sister but I didn't think they were ever going to be close. Ruth desperately wanted her brother to believe her but he just wanted to dish out blame.

As Liz left, Louisa came in from her friend's house, and Ruth couldn't wait to tell her the news.

'What happened at court?' she asked.

'My dad's going to prison because what he did was wrong.' She grinned.

'That's good,' said Louisa. 'Are you pleased?'

Ruth nodded.

She was still grinning from ear to ear when I tucked her in that night.

'I know I've said it before but I'm so proud of you,' I told her. 'And I hope you're proud of yourself.'

Ruth gave me a smile.

'Liz said she's coming round next week to have a chat with me about something,' she told me.

'Oh good,' I said.

I knew exactly what that was going to be about. Now the court case was over, it was time to tell Ruth about the fact that her biological mum was back on the scene and wanted to see her.

I had no idea how Ruth was going to react to the news. I hoped she was going to see it as a positive, but after everything she'd been through in the past few weeks, I wondered if it would be too much to cope with. We'd soon find out.

FOURTEEN

First Meetings

As promised, Liz came round the following week to break the news to Ruth about her biological mum. We'd already discussed how to play it. As a first step, Liz had got Sharon to write a letter to Ruth and one to David. Liz was going to tell Ruth about her mum and give the letter to her.

Ruth was still off school and we all sat round with a cup of tea in the front room.

'How have you been since the court case, Ruth?' asked Liz.

'Great.' She smiled. 'We went swimming yesterday and at the weekend we went up to the hills and had a picnic.'

'That sounds lovely,' she said.

Liz gave me a look that signalled the chit-chat was over and she was about to pass on the important news. I felt a bit apprehensive as neither of us was sure how Ruth was going to take it.

'Now then, Ruth,' said Liz, putting her hands in her lap and leaning towards her. 'I need to tell you something really serious and important.'

Ruth looked alarmed and I could tell that she was worried she was about to get told off.

'What?' she said. 'What is it?'

'I had a phone call from your birth mum Sharon a few months ago and she told me that she'd really, really like to get back in touch with you.'

Ruth's face fell and she looked shocked.

'She's given me a letter to give to you and I've got one for David too.'

Ruth didn't say a word as Liz handed her the envelope. It wasn't stuck down, and I knew Liz had probably read it first to check what Sharon had written.

Ruth quickly opened it up. It was a nice card with pretty pink flowers and cats on the front. I was sitting next to Ruth on the sofa so I could read what it said over her shoulder.

Dear Ruth, I hope you are well. I was so sad to hear what had happened to you. It would be really nice to meet up and be part of your life again. Can you talk to Liz and let her know if you'd like to meet me. Love Mum xxx

Liz had advised Sharon about what to say, and with children Ruth's age it was better to keep it short and simple rather than writing a long, emotional letter.

'Did you know about this?' Ruth asked me.

I knew I had to tell her the truth.

'Yes, I knew that your mum was back in contact,' I said. 'Liz and I went to see her to have a chat with her.'

'How come you didn't tell me?' she snapped, obviously annoyed by the fact that I had kept the news from her.

'Liz and I talked about it, but we didn't think it was the right time with the court case coming up. Sometimes adults have to make a decision and do what they think is best for a child.'

Thankfully Ruth didn't seem cross with me, but Liz got the brunt of her anger.

'You lied to me,' she said to her. 'How come you both went to see her and not me?'

'We didn't lie to you, Ruth,' said Liz. 'You had a lot to deal with and we wanted to meet your mum and talk to her, and check what kind of person she was before we introduced you.'

'Well, I don't think that's fair,' she said, angry tears filling her eyes. 'It's my mum.'

However, I could tell that Ruth was intrigued about her mum. She kept looking at the card and reading what it said.

'Where does she live?' she asked Liz.

'In a village in the countryside about three hours' drive from here,' she said.

'What's her house like?'

'It's a lovely little cottage,' Liz told her.

'I think you'd like it, Ruth,' I said. 'It's very cosy and your mum has got lots of rabbit ornaments that she collects.'

I could see her taking it all in.

'Has she got a dog?' she asked. 'What kind of car does she drive?'

'I'm afraid I've got no idea about her car and I don't think she has a dog,' said Liz. 'I don't remember seeing one when we went to visit her.'

'Has she got a bedroom for me?' asked Ruth. 'Is there a room for David too?'

Liz and I looked at each other. She already had the expectation that she was going to go and live with her mum and I knew we had to manage that. What surprised me was that Ruth hadn't asked where her mum had been all these years or why she'd left in the first place, which is what I'd have wanted to know. But I was an adult and Ruth had different priorities – most of them seemed to be about houses, pets and cars.

'Can you remember anything at all about your birth mum, Ruth?' Liz asked her.

Ruth closed her eyes and screwed up her face.

'Not much,' she sighed. 'I think I remember her taking us out to a café for fish and chips once, and she used to do my hair. I remember her putting bunches in my hair and I had bobbles with two little red balls on them, like cherries.'

It was interesting for me to hear this, as Ruth liked me to do her hair. Perhaps that was because of the vague memories of her mum doing the same.

'Your mum would like to phone you and say hello,' said Liz. 'How do you feel about that? Would you like to speak to her?'

'Have you got her number?' she asked. 'Can I phone her? I'll ring her now.'

'I'll arrange a date with your mum when I get back to the office and then I'll let you know when she's going to call. Does that sound OK?'

Ruth seemed very eager.

'Will it be tomorrow?' she said.

'Not tomorrow. But I promise it will be soon – probably sometime in the next few days. OK?'

Ruth nodded.

'I know your mum's excited about being in touch with you again,' said Liz. 'But this doesn't mean to say that you're going to go and live with her.'

I looked at Ruth and I could see that mentally she'd already packed her bags and moved in.

'We need to check that everything is OK first and that you're going to be happy,' I told her gently. 'You haven't seen your mum in years and you don't really know each other so we don't know how you're going to get on.'

'Well, I already know that I want to go and live with her,' said Ruth determinedly.

Liz and I looked at each other. So much for managing her expectations.

I hoped for her sake that things worked out, I really did. Otherwise she was going to be totally and utterly devastated.

When Liz had gone, Ruth went into the kitchen and I heard her telling Lily about what had happened.

'My real mum sent me a card,' she said. 'I'm going to go and live with her in her big house and she's got a posh car, too.'

'That's nice,' said Lily, who wasn't remotely interested.

By the time I was serving up dinner that night and Ruth was relaying the story to Louisa, the exaggeration had escalated.

'My mum's house has six bedrooms and she's even got a swimming pool in the garden,' she boasted.

I knew I had to step in.

'Ruth, when I went to see her I think there were only two bedrooms and I'm pretty sure she didn't have a pool.'

'Yeah, well, that's not her real house,' she said.

Ruth wasn't prepared to hear the truth. She was building up this picture of her mum in her head – this perfect woman who was going to whisk her away to this wonderful life. I only hoped the reality wasn't going to be too much of a disappointment.

'Does her mum really live in a mansion?' Louisa asked me later as we cleared away the dishes.

I shook my head, but I knew I couldn't shoot down Ruth's dreams. She'd come to me with nothing, she'd lost everything and now here was her mum – back in her life and wanting to see her. I couldn't burst her bubble. I knew that sometimes kids had to invent a fantasy in order to be able to cope with how things really were and I hoped that over time Ruth would get used to the reality.

That night Ruth had lots more questions about her mum for me.

'What did you say to her when you met her?' she asked.

'We talked about you. I told her what you liked doing and how you were getting on at school.

'I took her some photos of you and she was really pleased. She already had a picture of you in a frame that was taken when you were little.'

'Did she?' She grinned.

'She's obviously never stopped thinking about you and wondering how you were,' I told her.

I could see that she liked the idea of that.

'Has she got any pets?' she asked.

'She's got three cats,' I said.

'I bet she's got a dog too,' said Ruth. 'And rabbits. I bet she's got rabbits hopping around her big garden.'

'If you say so, although she didn't mention it to me.' I smiled.

Amazingly, Ruth didn't seem to have any anger, bitterness or resentment towards her mum. What she did have were these huge expectations and I hoped she wasn't going to be too disappointed.

A couple of days later, as promised, Liz set up a phone call between Ruth and Sharon. Ruth was hyped up with excitement and spent the morning dancing around the phone. When it finally rang, she froze and let me answer it.

'Hello, Sharon,' I said. 'I've got Ruth standing right here, waiting to talk to you, so I'll pass you over.'

'Thank you so much,' she said.

She sounded excited and nervous.

'Hello,' said Ruth warily.

I hovered in the background as Liz had asked me to stay in the room while they were talking, in case Ruth got upset or needed rescuing. But she seemed fine and happily bombarded poor Sharon with endless questions: 'What car have you got? When are you coming up? What job do you do? What is your house like? How many bedrooms does it have? Will you buy me some new clothes?'

She was coming across as very materialistic, and I hoped it didn't put Sharon off. I knew Ruth's cockiness was her protection for when she was feeling vulnerable, but her mum didn't know that.

They chatted for ten minutes and Ruth was grinning like a Cheshire cat when she came off the phone.

'My mum says she's going to ask Liz if she can come up and see me, and she's going to bring me a present.'

'That's lovely,' I said, unsure whether to believe her or not, as I hadn't been able to hear what Sharon had been saying. Ruth seemed happy enough with the way it had gone, though.

While she was watching telly, I nipped upstairs and gave Liz a call. I knew that Sharon was due to phone her after her conversation with Ruth and tell her how it had gone.

'How did Mum find the phone call?' I asked nervously.

'She was really happy,' said Liz. 'She thought Ruth was absolutely delightful and that she sounded lovely.'

'Really?' I said, shocked. 'I thought she came across as a little bit spoilt.'

Both Liz and I burst out laughing.

'I can always rely on you to speak the truth, Maggie,' she said.

We chatted a bit more.

'How was Ruth afterwards?' asked Liz. 'Was she upset or distressed?'

'Not in the slightest,' I said. 'She can't wait to see her mum and get the present that she promised her.'

To Ruth, her mum was the best thing since sliced bread, and her two-bed house was a mansion. Nothing anybody said was going to change that.

Over the next few days, Ruth was full of talk about the amazing present her mum was going to get for her.

'I wonder what she's bringing me?' she asked about ten times a day.

She talked about the things they were going to do when her mum came up, like going shopping and to the cinema and having a meal in a fancy restaurant. I could see her trying to bait Louisa and Lily with her boasts and make them jealous. But both of them were happy for her and weren't in the least bit bothered.

In the meantime, Liz and I sat down and discussed how the next few weeks were going to play out.

'I've organised with Sharon that she's going to come over to the family centre once a week for the next five weeks on her day off and spend a couple of hours with Ruth,' she said. 'If eventually it does look like Ruth wants to move in with her then we'll build up the contact and I've warned her that she might need to take more time off work.'

'Is she willing to do that?' I asked.

'Oh, she's willing to do whatever it takes to get her kids back,' said Liz. 'But she knows we have to take things slowly at first.

'I've said that if the initial contacts go well then she can ring Ruth once a week too.'

Ruth's first few meetings with her mum were going to take place at a family centre attached to the Social Services offices. There were several different rooms and a kitchen there.

'Sharon's obviously not a threat and we're not worried about her, but I'm going to supervise the first contact to check Ruth's OK with it, and then we can see how it goes from there,' she said.

'What about David?' I asked. 'Are they going to see Sharon together or separately?'

'Ah, I wanted to talk to you about that,' said Liz.

She explained that David had reacted very differently from Ruth when she'd told him about their mum getting back in touch.

'He didn't take it well at all,' she said. 'He's very angry and resentful towards Mum for leaving them, and he was adamant that he doesn't want to see her or have anything to do with her.

'I don't want to push him. He's older than Ruth and it's his decision, so it's just Ruth in the picture for now.'

In a way, I thought David's response was more natural and honest than Ruth's. He was quite right to be angry with his mother – the fact was she *had* left them. Part of me wanted Ruth to be angry with her too, so we could work through it now rather than it come up later down the line and cause more of a problem. However, in a way, I was glad David wasn't interested in seeing their mum. I knew Ruth would benefit from having one-to-one contact with Sharon without having to worry about what her brother was doing or thinking.

On the day that Ruth was due to meet her mum for the first time, I finally told her it was happening. I never tell children that they're seeing their parents right up until the last moment as plans often change and it's best to avoid the disappointment.

'Liz has arranged for you to see your mum today,' I told her.

She was excited but also very nervous.

'What will I say to her?' she asked. 'What if I don't like her?'

'Don't worry,' I reassured her. 'Liz will be there to make sure that you're happy.

'I'm sure you will like her but if you don't or you decide you don't want to see her again then that's fine. Just tell Liz. It's completely up to you.'

'Can I bring the card she sent me?' she asked.

'If you want to,' I said.

I wasn't sure why she wanted to take the card, but I think she wanted to show her mum that she'd still got it and that it was important to her.

'Do you want to take some photographs to show her?' I asked.

Like all of the children I fostered, Ruth had an album filled with lots of pictures of the things we'd done over the past few months since she'd come to live with me.

'No thanks,' she said. 'I'll be too busy opening all my presents to look at stupid pictures.'

Mum's present had now been exaggerated into a whole room full of gifts.

In the car on the way there, Ruth was fidgety and couldn't keep still.

'Remember, Liz is there for you,' I said. 'If you feel uncomfortable or you want to cut things short, then tell her. It's completely your choice. Nobody's going to force you to do anything that you don't want to do.'

'I know,' she said. 'I think I'm going to like her, though.'

'Well, that's good then,' I said. 'I just want you to know that you have choices.'

As we walked into the family centre, Ruth saw Liz and ran over to her.

'Where is she?' she asked. 'Is she here yet?'

'Not yet,' said Liz. 'How about we go to the kitchen and make ourselves a drink and by then I'm sure she'll have arrived.'

Liz gave me a look and I knew exactly what we were both thinking.

Please, please don't let her pull out. Please let her turn up.

I'd dealt with so many parents over the years who swore blind they were coming to the contact meeting. You'd ring them to check and they'd say they were just about to get into their car or on a bus but then they would never show. It was always devastating for the kids and I wasn't sure Ruth would be able to cope with the disappointment.

Liz and I had already decided that it probably wasn't a good idea for me to stay for the contact. I didn't want to be seen as a barrier between Ruth and her mum – either for Ruth to think she was being disloyal or Sharon to see me as a threat.

'I'm going to go now,' I said to Ruth. 'I hope you have a lovely time with your mum.'

'I will.' She smiled.

As I pulled out of the car park, I breathed a sigh of relief as I saw Sharon driving in. I was so pleased that she'd kept her word. She smiled as she passed me and I gave her a wave. What amused me was that I noticed she was driving a battered old banger, while Ruth had been boasting about her posh car to everyone.

She's not going to like that, I thought to myself as I drove home.

Liz dropped Ruth back a couple of hours later. She bounded into the house, as high as a kite.

'How did it go?' I asked her.

'Look what my mum bought me,' she said, showing me a bangle and some gold, heart-shaped stud earrings.

'What a lovely thoughtful present,' I said. 'They're beautiful.'

I was pleased that Sharon hadn't gone over the top and spent a fortune trying to win Ruth over with expensive gifts.

'I didn't bring the other presents home because there was so many of them,' she told me. 'My mum's going to take them back to her house and keep them in my bedroom there.'

I knew there probably weren't any other presents but Ruth obviously felt the need to exaggerate.

'Well, that's great about the presents,' I said. 'But never mind those, what did you think to your mum? Did you like her?'

'Oh, she was beautiful.' Ruth smiled. 'She wears such nice clothes and lovely make-up. She's so posh.'

It was a totally different image from the mousy, plain woman that Liz and I had met, but whatever Ruth had seen in Sharon, it had obviously made her very happy.

'And, Maggie, you was right, she has got cats, but she says when I go and live with her I can have a dog.'

I hoped that it had gone as well as she was making out, but I knew I needed to ring Liz to get the real story.

'How did it go?' I asked her.

'They were both quiet to start off with,' she said. 'Mum was tearful and emotional to see Ruth, but Ruth seemed fine.

'She didn't say much at first and it was a bit awkward and stilted. But I made small talk and eventually they started to chat to each other.

'Ruth loved the present that Sharon had bought her and she was very appreciative. She asked lots of questions again – mainly about possessions – but Mum seemed to take it well and at the end they gave each other a hug when they said goodbye.'

'Well, Ruth is besotted by her,' I said. 'She keeps asking me when she can go and live with her.

'Do you still think that's what Sharon wants?'

'She says so,' said Liz. 'Obviously, she has to go through a full assessment first and I'm keen to slow the process right down.'

Sharon would have to go through what Social Services called a parenting assessment to make sure this wasn't going to go wrong for Ruth. They'd already done checks that had shown she wasn't known to the police or Social Services. As well as the contact visits, Sharon would have to have regular meetings with Liz and talk about Ruth and how she'd handle certain situations and behaviours.

'How do you feel about the possibility of her going to live with her mum?' Liz asked me.

'Honestly, I'm really pleased for her,' I said. 'I think it's the best possible outcome for Ruth.'

I'd always known my role had been to see her through the court case, and only then were we going to look at long-term plans. Although I'd grown very fond of Ruth, the tension she created in the house with Louisa and Lily sometimes was hard to live with and it hadn't been easy. We'd all softened to her and grown to love her, and although I'd be sad to see her go, I knew being with her mum would be good for her. She needed that one-to-one attention and I knew she'd thrive on that.

'I hope that Sharon is serious about taking this forward,' I said. 'If she isn't and she pulls out, then it's going to be absolutely devastating for Ruth.'

I also hoped that she genuinely cared for her daughter and wasn't just motivated by guilt. I hoped she did want to be with Ruth and give her the love, care and security she hadn't had so far in her childhood.

If she did, it could be the best thing to ever happen to Ruth. But I knew there were many hurdles to face on the way.

All the excitement about meeting her mum had enabled Ruth to put the court case to the back of her mind. However, I knew that soon it would be time for her dad to appear back in court to be sentenced.

Liz rang me a few days beforehand.

'Do you want to come to court for the sentencing?' she asked.

I hadn't even reminded Ruth that it was happening as she was so caught up in meeting her mum. I felt that bringing up the sentencing with her would make her take a step back and only remind her of the stress of the court case.

'Ruth hasn't mentioned it at all,' I said. 'So I'm more than happy for you to go.'

'OK,' said Liz. 'Obviously, I'll ring you straight afterwards and let you know the outcome.'

It was around eleven the next morning when the phone rang.

'He got nine years,' said Liz. 'Can you believe it?'

She was delighted and she said the police were too, as that was more than they'd hoped for. He'd also be on the Sex Offender Register for life.

'The judge told him it was a despicable thing that he had done, abusing his own daughter and destroying her childhood.'

'Did her dad kick off again?' I asked.

'Nope,' she said. 'He just shook his head as he was led away.'

'Do you want to break the news to Ruth or do you want me to pop round and do it?' she asked.

'If it's OK with you, I'm happy to tell her,' I said.

'That's fine by me,' she said.

Rather than sitting Ruth down and making a big deal out of it, I decided to tell her in a casual, low-key way. That night, we were washing up after dinner and there were just the two of us in the kitchen. Sometimes, with kids, it's good to pass on important information like this when you're involved in a task and you haven't got eye contact. It puts less pressure and stress on them and sometimes they feel that they can talk more freely. Children can tell you the most important things at the strangest times. I remember one child that I'd fostered telling me he'd been sexually abused by his grandad completely out of the blue when I was taking roast potatoes out of the oven.

'Liz rang today,' I said casually, passing her a wet plate to dry. 'She said the judge has sent your dad to prison for nine years.'

'Oh,' said Ruth.

'And you know that he's been put away because everybody believed you,' I said, trying to reiterate the message. 'Also, he'll have to go on a special register that means he won't be able to live in the same house as a child under sixteen for the rest of his life.'

'That's good then,' she said.

I carried on with washing a couple of mugs to give her a chance to take on board what I'd told her.

'How do you feel about that?' I asked eventually.

'Dunno.' She shrugged. 'I just don't want to see him.'

'You will never have to see him again,' I said. 'He's safely locked away and he's going to be behind bars for a long, long time.'

Like Ruth, I wasn't sure how I felt about the sentence either. Neither of us was jumping for joy. In my mind, the most important thing was that he'd been found guilty, which proved to Ruth that everyone believed her. I was glad that her dad had gone to prison, but how long he'd got was almost irrelevant to me.

'Does David know about Dad?' she asked.

'Yes, Liz will be telling him,' I said.

'I don't want to see him this time, though,' she told me.

'That's fine,' I said. 'But why's that?'

'He's been horrible about Mum. She told me. He didn't like her card and he's angry at her and doesn't want to see her.'

'At the end of the day, David will do what he needs to do,' I told her. 'As long as you're happy and you want to see your mum, then that's fine.'

'I am sure and I am happy,' she said. 'I want to go and live with her now.'

'And hopefully you will,' I told her. 'You've just got to be patient while the adults work everything out.'

The excitement of being reunited with her mum had finally taken away the worry and fear that the court case had caused, and that was fine by me.

FIFTEEN

Opening Up

Ruth had been back at school over a couple of weeks now. I'd promised to keep the head teacher Mr Mattison up to date with the events in Ruth's life, so I arranged to go and see him.

'How did the trial go?' he asked.

'Thankfully her dad was found guilty and he got nine years,' I said.

'Good,' he said. 'I bet that's a relief.'

I nodded.

'And how's Ruth feeling about it all?'

'She's OK,' I said. 'She coped brilliantly with giving her evidence in court, and although there have been a few wobbles along the way, she's doing remarkably well, considering.

'There have also been a few other developments that I wanted to talk to you about.'

I explained how Ruth was back in touch with her biological mum.

'They've met up a couple of times and if all continues to go well then we're looking at the possibility of Ruth going to live with her permanently,' I said.

'I'm really pleased for her, but do you think it's going to work out?' he asked.

He knew how challenging Ruth could be and how she'd behaved when she'd first come to live with me. She was very amenable now but what if, under stress, she reverted to her old ways? Could Sharon cope with that? At the moment they were both trying desperately hard to please each other and it was all going a bit too smoothly in my opinion.

'They both seem to want this but you can never predict what's going to happen,' I said. 'I know it will be a steep learning curve for both of them.'

Even though we'd told Sharon about how Ruth used to be and spoken honestly about her negative behaviour, Sharon was so desperate to have her daughter back that I'm not sure she'd taken it on board. She was, however, passing all her assessments and attending all the contact sessions so there wasn't much more we could do.

'Ruth doesn't know it yet but she's also about to start counselling,' I said. 'The sessions will be after school but it's going to be pretty intensive and hard going so I wanted to let you know in case there's any sudden change in her behaviour.'

'Thanks for the heads-up,' he said. 'I think it would be helpful for you to stay in touch and let us know if she's having a particularly bad time so we can make allowances.

'I wouldn't want to come down hard on her if she's really going through it again.'

'Thank you,' I said. 'I appreciate that.'

It was so helpful having a supportive head teacher like Mr Mattison on board who genuinely cared.

Now I knew I had to raise the idea of counselling with Ruth. Because of the court case, for months we'd actively encouraged her not to talk about her dad or the abuse and now we were going completely the other way, so I wasn't sure how she was going to feel.

Liz and I had agreed it would be a good idea to get Sharon involved too. She and Ruth had had two contact visits now. On the second one they'd spent an hour at the family centre with Liz, to check that Ruth was happy, then they'd gone into town for some lunch.

'How did it go?' I'd asked Ruth when she came back that afternoon. 'Was it nice spending some time on your own with your mum?'

'It was great,' she'd said. 'We went and looked for clothes and I showed her what I wanted for Christmas.'

Before I mentioned the therapy, I wanted to check that she was genuinely happy about Mum.

'How are you feeling about things? I asked her. 'Are you pleased with the way it's going?'

Ruth nodded.

'Do you ever ask your mum why she left?' I said.

'She wasn't keen on my dad, but she doesn't like to talk about it a lot,' she told me.

Liz had already raised the possibility with Sharon of her taking part in some of the counselling sessions with Ruth, and also having some time with the same therapist on her own. I agreed that this was necessary as there were so many unexplored issues. Mum was carrying guilt about the past and Ruth was so grateful that someone wanted her that she didn't want to do anything to put Sharon off. Therapy would help them work through some of the issues that were likely to pop up later and cause problems.

'Liz and I both want you to go back to live with your mum if that's what you want,' I said. 'But you haven't had the opportunity to talk about everything that's happened and how you're feeling with someone.'

'Talk about what?' asked Ruth.

'What's happened with your dad, meeting your mum again. That kind of thing,' I said. 'Liz and I have found this really nice place where you can go and talk to someone once a week for a few months and see how it goes.'

Ruth looked at me suspiciously.

'What place?' she asked. 'Where is it?'

'It's only about half an hour away from here,' I said. 'We can go and have a look round next week.

'You'll chat to someone called a counsellor and she'll try to help you work through things.'

'What's she going to do?'

'She'll do anything you want to,' I said. 'If you want to paint, you can do paintings. If you want to draw flowers, you can draw flowers. And if you get there and you don't want to talk about anything, then that's fine too.

'We just thought it would be useful for you to chat to someone other than Liz and me. Does that sound OK?'

Ruth nodded, but I could tell she wasn't entirely convinced.

A couple of days later we arranged to go and look around the children's centre with Liz. It was a brand spanking new building that had only been open just over a year. It was very swish with lots of glass and sliding doors, which Ruth loved. We sat in the reception area and waited for the therapist to come and meet us.

'It's posh, isn't it?' whispered Ruth.

Everything was white, clinical and new. Eventually a woman came over to us. She was tall, with long, blonde hair and a flowing skirt and brown sandals that meant you could see the rings on her toes.

'Hello, I'm Liberty,' she beamed. 'And you must be Ruth.'

I could see Ruth liked her straight away.

'I love your jewellery,' Ruth said, taking in the various earrings in Liberty's ears and the huge amber pendant she was wearing. She was warm and smiley, and I was pleased that Ruth seemed so taken with her.

She showed us around all the different rooms. Some had sofas in them with piles of books and toys, while others were set up with easels and big tables with paints, scissors and crayons all over them.

'Which one will I be in?' asked Ruth.

'You can go into whichever room you fancy,' Liberty told her.

'What do we have to talk about?' she said.

'Whatever you want,' Liberty said. 'We can talk about your dad or mum or Liz or Maggie. Absolutely anything.

'Or we don't even have to talk – we can just get a cup of tea.'

'I don't drink tea,' said Ruth with a scowl.

Despite her wariness, though, I could see that Ruth liked Liberty and her jangly bangles and positive, sunny attitude.

Liz and I met up later that week and agreed that Ruth would have one two-hour session a week for three months.

'Mum's going to get involved with the sessions halfway through,' said Liz. 'If all goes well then at the end of the three months we can look at Ruth going to live with Sharon permanently.'

'What about contact?' I asked.

'We'll start to increase that as well,' she said. 'Once the first five sessions have finished Ruth can go and do an overnight at her mum's and then we'll build that up to a weekend.'

I felt three months was long enough to assess whether everything was OK and everyone was happy.

I hoped the counselling would help Ruth and she went willingly to her first session.

'How did it go?' I asked her when I went to pick her up.

'Great,' she beamed. 'I ate loads of chocolate biscuits and drank orange squash. I finished off the whole packet and Liberty didn't even tell me off.'

I suspected that Ruth wouldn't do much talking for the first couple of sessions. But this changed as the therapy progressed.

It was a nice sunny evening after her third session so I decided to walk the half an hour to the centre to collect her. As Ruth walked towards me I could tell straight away by her demeanor that things were different this time around. After the first couple of sessions she'd skipped to the car when I'd come to pick her up. This time, she walked slowly and laboriously.

'Did you find it hard today?' I asked gently.

'Yes,' she said, looking at the ground.

I was careful not to ask Ruth too many questions, as she'd been there for over an hour, but I wanted her to know that I was there for her.

'If you want to tell me what happened with Liberty today then you know you can,' I said.

'We were talking about my dad,' she told me as we walked along. 'About how I felt when I was little.'

I didn't say anything and let her continue.

'I could remember really clearly in my head being little and him hurting me and it made me feel scared.'

Ruth suddenly seemed like a terrified child again and even though her dad was locked away, I could see he continued to have power over her. I reached out for her hand.

'He can't hurt you any more,' I said.

Ruth didn't say anything else and we walked home in silence, holding hands.

'Maggie, can I have a bath?' she asked as soon as we got through the front door.

'Of course you can,' I said.

I was surprised as I normally had to remind her to have a wash and she always preferred a quick shower to a bath. But I could see that talking about her dad and what he'd done to her had made her feel horrible and ashamed about herself, and it was as if she wanted to wash it all away.

'Please can you do my hair?' she asked me afterwards.

That had always been her way of seeking out comfort from me.

'How about a French plait?' I said.

I sat behind her on the settee and brushed her long, dark hair and started dividing it into sections. I'd been doing it for ten minutes, chatting idly away to her, when she suddenly said: 'I don't know why he did it to me. I know I was naughty sometimes but I wasn't as bad as he made out. I was only little. I didn't deserve that.'

I didn't say anything as I was so pleased that she was opening up to me. I just ran my fingers through her hair so, although she couldn't see me, she knew that I was there and I was listening.

'I thought it was my fault for ages. That I'd done something to make him be like that but I know now what he did was wrong.

'He was my dad so he should have looked after me, shouldn't he? It wasn't my fault.'

She burst into tears. Big, gulping sobs that made her whole body shake.

'It's OK,' I soothed, carrying on stroking her hair. 'It's OK, Ruth. I'm here. I can't imagine how horrible that must have been for you, but you're safe now.'

'Please can I have a tissue?' she snivelled and I passed her one.

'You're being very brave,' I told her.

She nodded.

'Are you going to carry on doing my hair, or not?' she demanded and I smiled.

As I put a bobble in the end of the plait to secure it, I knew this was an enormous breakthrough for Ruth to be opening up to me about her dad and the abuse. I knew her well enough by now to know that the best thing to do was to sit back, not ask too many questions and let her go at her own pace. I couldn't even begin to understand how hard it must be for her.

That night I could see she was exhausted and she went to bed early. The next morning she was still in such a deep sleep that I struggled to wake her.

After she left for school, I phoned Mr Mattison.

'I wanted to let you know that Ruth had a bit of a rough counselling session yesterday,' I said. 'She's very tired this morning so a bit of leeway might be needed today.'

'No problem,' he said. 'I'll let her teachers know.'

That became our routine. I'd pick Ruth up from counselling and we'd walk back home together and chat.

'Would you like me to do your hair tonight?' I'd ask.

'No.' She'd smile. 'It wasn't a bad one today.'

I could see that she was working through everything in her head. All the years of abuse, all that hurt and pain came tumbling out. Understandably it was overwhelming and confusing for her at times.

After another particularly gruelling therapy session, Ruth handed me the hairbrush when we got home. She didn't respond well to eye contact and hugs but she seemed to feel comfortable opening up to me when she had her back to me and I was fiddling with her hair.

'Sometimes I get really confused,' she said. 'I know what my dad did was wrong, but after he hurt me he was nice to me and gave me sweets and fizzy pop.

'No one was ever kind to me or gave me treats or stuff like that so sometimes I didn't mind putting up with it if it meant I got nice things afterwards. But that was wrong, wasn't it?'

Poor, poor girl, having to go through this unbearable cruelty for so many years.

'When he was hurting me I used to shut my eyes and pretend I was somewhere else. Somewhere nice like at a fair or going on a plane.'

'You were just a little girl and what he did was wrong,' I said. 'It's not your fault.'

I kept on telling her that and slowly Ruth started to accept it. As each week passed and she talked more and more about her feelings and the abuse, she seemed physically lighter. She started walking back from therapy with her head up and I could even see the change in the artwork that she brought home.

She often came back with items she had made or paintings that she'd done. In the kitchen there was a big cork board on the wall and Lily would regularly come home from school and get a painting or a drawing she'd done out of her book bag. She'd pin it up and I'd ask her to tell me about it and praise her. After therapy one afternoon Ruth came home and got a painting out of her bag and pinned it up on the board. The picture was mainly black with a dark sky and lots of rain.

'Oh,' I said, unsure what to say. 'That's interesting.'

Ruth scowled and the message was clear – don't talk to me about it. But she had obviously wanted me to see it.

The next few pictures she brought home were the same – everything was dark, moody and destructive. But as the therapy progressed her paintings started to change. They were never of people but there were abstract blobs of bright colours, dazzling blues and greens and vivid pinks. She would ask me what I thought of them and she obviously wanted me to comment on these pictures and praise her.

'Those colours are beautiful,' I said. 'What a lovely picture. I can see you've worked very hard on that.'

Ruth might have been twelve years old but she was like a little girl, handing me her artwork and waiting for me to heap praise on her. She was trying to be the child who went home to a dad and a loving, caring family who were proud of her and the pictures she'd drawn, but she'd missed out on all of that.

I'd no idea what the therapist made of them but I loved seeing the pictures on the board go from doom and gloom to bright and alive. It showed me that Ruth was letting go of the past and finally moving forward.

The therapy seemed to be helping and after four sessions Liberty thought it would be a good idea to get Sharon involved.

Contact between the two of them was still going well. Sharon had taken Ruth to a farm for an afternoon and they'd been to a theme park for the day, which Ruth had loved.

'We thought it would be good for your mum to come to your next therapy session,' I told Ruth.

But she didn't seem too happy with the idea.

'Why's she got to interfere with what I'm doing? It's my time with Liberty, not hers.'

'We thought it would be helpful for both of you to talk to her,' I said.

Ruth seemed to come round to the idea and Liz thought it might be nice for Sharon to come to my house to collect Ruth so they could walk to the family centre together.

'That's not a problem,' I told Liz. 'But I'd like Sharon to come in and have a cup of tea with us beforehand.'

I was worried that Ruth would find it hard having us both around and might feel the need to show off or throw a strop on the doorstep.

'I'm happy with that and I think it would be good for Ruth to see you and Sharon together,' she said. 'Then it's almost like you're giving her permission to be with her mum and showing her that you're OK with that.'

Ruth appeared to like the idea too.

'I'm going to make her a special invite asking her to come round,' she said.

She spent hours drawing a card for Sharon. It had a table on the front with cups of tea and cake on it and inside she'd written:

To my mum, please come for tea and cake on Saturday at 2, luv Ruth xxxoo

Their counselling session didn't start until 4 p.m. so Sharon would be at the house for two hours. I crossed my fingers that Ruth wouldn't play up and we'd have plenty to talk about.

I suggested that we posted the card to Sharon as a surprise. I gave Ruth the address and she copied it out carefully on an envelope.

'This will be my new address when I go and live with Mum.' She smiled.

I hoped she was right.

On the morning of the day that Sharon was coming round, Ruth and Lily were in the kitchen. When I came in, I saw they'd emptied out my baking drawer and there were mixing bowls, sprinkles and bun cases all over the floor.

'Instead of buying cakes for my mum, please can Lily and I make them?' Ruth asked with big pleading eyes.

'Go on then.' I smiled.

'I know how to do it,' said Lily.

I got them set up then I made a cup of tea and went into the other room.

'Call me if you need me and I'll come back and put them in the oven for you,' I said, leaving them to it, as they seemed determined to do it by themselves.

I went into the living room and sat down in a chair with one ear out listening to the conversations that were taking place in the kitchen.

'Are you sure it's a whole bag of sugar, Lily?'

'Only one egg?'

'Why do we need yogurt?'

At that point I leapt up and talked them through the recipe so they knew exactly what ingredients to put into the bowl. I was all for kids taking ownership of a task but I couldn't bear the thought of Sharon coming round and having to eat awful cakes.

After helping them measure everything out, I left them to it again. There was a lot of banging and clattering coming from the kitchen and I could hear them chatting.

'Do you like your mum?' I heard Lily ask Ruth.

'Yeah, she's OK.'

'Are you going to go and live with her?'

'I think so.'

'Will you miss us?'

'Nah.'

'Yes you will, and I will miss you.'

The exchange between the two of them was open and honest, and it was fascinating. However, I knew it was time to step in again when I heard the next bit.

'I don't think we need green food colouring, Ruth.'

'Lily, why are you putting salt in it?'

I ran into the kitchen. Thankfully the cake mixture wasn't green and there was no sign of any salt.

'Right, I'll help you get them in the cases and pop them in the oven,' I said.

A few hours later the cakes were cooked and decorated, and Sharon was due to arrive. When she got there, it was nice to see Ruth giving her a hug and there seemed to be genuine affection between them.

'Hello again,' she said.

She looked nervous. I hadn't seen her since Liz and I had gone down to meet her. I felt it was important for her to realise that I wasn't a threat and that I was happy that Ruth wanted to go and live with her. It was also good for Ruth to see her mum and me getting on and to know that I didn't think she was being disloyal by wanting to be with her.

Ruth couldn't wait for Sharon to see her handiwork.

'Ta-da,' she said, showing her the plates of fairy cakes that amazingly had turned out fine. 'I made them with Lily.'

'Wow, they look great,' said Sharon. 'Aren't you clever?'

It was lovely to see Ruth's smile at being praised.

Ruth showed Sharon round the house and took her up to see her bedroom. It was important for Sharon to see where her daughter had lived for the past nine months.

Then we all sat and had a cup of tea and a cake. I noticed Ruth had already wolfed a couple of them down in minutes and when I saw her reach out for her third, I was about to say something but I stopped myself. I wanted to wait and see if Sharon would say anything, but she didn't.

'Ruth, I think three cakes is more than enough,' I said. 'You'll make yourself sick. If you're still hungry get yourself an apple.'

I was worried that Ruth had control in their relationship and not Sharon. Sharon was so eager to please her daughter that she didn't want to stand up to her, but I knew from experience that Ruth needed firm boundaries.

I told myself it wasn't fair to judge Sharon on that one incident. Perhaps she didn't feel it was her place to tell Ruth off in my house. I did hope, however, that Sharon would soon take the reins of control and assert her authority over her daughter, otherwise things could quickly break down.

SIXTEEN

Progress and Plans

The front door slammed shut and Ruth stomped into the kitchen with the biggest grin on her face.

'Ask me what happened at school today.' she said.

'OK,' I replied. 'What *did* happen at school today?'

'I got chosen for the netball team.' She beamed. 'I'm going to be the centre.'

'Wow, that's brilliant,' I said, completely surprised. 'Well done.'

I hadn't even known that Ruth liked netball or was any good at it.

'One of the girls has broken her arm and she can't play so they needed someone for the rest of the term,' she said. 'I had to try out at lunchtime and they picked me.

'Will you come and watch me play?'

'Of course I will,' I said. 'I bet Louisa and Lily will want to come too.'

That weekend there was a home game so the three of us went up to school to cheer her on. I was a bit nervous about how she was going to cope but I was gobsmacked at how good she was. I watched in amazement as Ruth tore up and down the court, passing the ball to her teammates. When she got a goal, we all whooped and cheered from the sidelines.

'Go, Ruthie Ruth!' yelled Lily, and Ruth grinned with pride.

I knew it was a huge thing for Ruth to be able to play as part of a team. For someone who had always struggled to make friends, it was a big deal. To her it felt like she'd finally been accepted and, to my surprise, she looked like she fitted in. She knew the rules and what she was supposed to be doing, she chatted away to the other girls and she was clearly enjoying herself.

Mr Mattison was there too and when he saw me in the crowd, he came over for a chat.

'When did you swap Ruth?' he asked.

'What do you mean?' I laughed.

'Well, the amenable, productive girl we've got coming to school at the moment is nothing like the Ruth who first started here,' he said.

'I know,' I said. 'And, believe you me, the new improved version is so much easier to live with.'

He told me how Ruth was concentrating in class and getting on with her work, and that she was cheerful and polite. Her behaviour had always been manageable at this school but she was one of those pupils whose name would elicit a groan from any teacher. But now none of them could believe how much she'd changed.

'She's like a different person since the trial ended and she started counselling,' I said.

She was starting to have confidence in herself and build up some self-esteem.

'Look at her,' I said, as she ran up and down the netball pitch. 'She's loving it out there.'

When Ruth came off the court, sweaty but happy, I gave her a big hug.

'You were absolutely brilliant,' I told her. 'And so fast. I never knew you were so good at netball.'

'You were great,' said Lily. 'You were jumping up so high. Do you want to join my gymnastics class?'

'No thanks, Lily,' said Ruth and we all laughed.

Ruth had come so far yet there were still a few unresolved issues that I felt we needed to address before she went to live with her mum. One of those was food.

No matter how hard I'd worked with Ruth, her fear that there wouldn't be any food for her meant that she still had problems in this area. I must admit I'd taken my eye off the ball a bit as I thought things had been resolved. One day after school, however, I was proved wrong. I noticed that Lily had only eaten half of her pasta bake.

'I'll tidy the plates away,' Ruth announced, jumping up as she always did to help clear the table.

I watched her walk over to the bin. When she thought no one was looking, she bent down and shoved huge handfuls of leftover pasta into her mouth.

I started to keep a closer eye on what was left at the end of a meal and I even began checking the bin. Even after all this time, Ruth was eating anything left over on anyone's plate. Nothing went into the bin. It was all being secretly shovelled into her mouth as she cleared away.

I'd reassured her time after time that food would always be available and that she would never go without a meal or feel hungry. I took her shopping to the supermarket so she would see the trolley full of food and she'd help me unpack it at home so she saw it all going into the cupboards. However, she still had this deep-seated anxiety.

I was at a loss about how to move forward with it. Ruth wasn't overweight, in fact she'd been too skinny when she'd first come to live with me. However, as the months had passed she'd filled out and grown taller. The black shadows under her eyes had gone and she had colour in her cheeks for the first time. She looked healthy but I knew her attitude to food wasn't and I wanted to try and change that before she moved in with her mum and it got worse or caused a problem.

The other kids had also started to comment on it. Lily came running into the living room after tea one night.

'Ugh, Maggie, Ruth's doing it again. She's eating all the scraps off the dinner plates.'

'No I weren't, you tell-tale rat,' she yelled from the kitchen.

Other times, if Lily or Louisa caught Ruth eating leftovers or rooting around in the bin, Ruth would drop a plate on the floor to cause a distraction.

I was watching TV late one evening when Ruth suddenly appeared next to me.

'What are you doing downstairs?' I asked her. 'You should be in bed at this time.'

'Maggie, I'm hungry and I can't sleep,' she moaned.

I knew she couldn't possibly be hungry as she'd had a huge tea but I didn't want her to start taking food from the cupboards again and hiding it in her bedroom.

So I put three apples into a bowl and handed it to her.

'Here, take this up to your room and keep it on your chest of drawers,' I said.

In the morning she brought the bowl downstairs and it was empty. I hoped that having a fruit bowl in her room would help reassure her that food was always available, even in the middle of the night, and that she'd gradually wean herself off it.

One night when I was curling her hair for her, I thought I'd try to talk to her about it. It was at times like this she seemed the most responsive and willing to open up to me.

'You know when you lived with your stepmum and your dad, did you all sit down and eat together or would you ever go out for meals?'

Ruth shook her head.

'If my mum thought I'd been bad or there were jobs I hadn't done that day, she'd send me to bed with no lunch or tea.'

'You poor thing,' I said. 'You must have been hungry then?'

'Sometimes I'd get up in the middle of the night and eat stuff out of the bin. That way, my mum wouldn't tell me off the next morning when she checked to see if any food was missing from the cupboards.'

I could see where her confused view of food had come from. She'd been denied meals and left to go hungry, and then her dad had plied her with sweets and treats as a reward after he'd abused her.

I decided to pick Liz's brain and see if she could help. I'd been passing bits and bobs to her about Ruth's eating in my daily notes but I wanted to talk to her about it in more detail.

'It's something we've both been aware of, on and off,' I said. 'But it hasn't gone away and when Ruth goes to live with her mum I don't want it to become a big issue.'

I explained how she'd been eating leftovers and taking food from the bin. How she was always the first to finish even when

I served her last and how she was obsessed with watching people eat.

'Don't get me wrong, things have improved since she first came,' I said. 'She's not taking food from downstairs and hiding it in her bedroom any more.'

Liz said Ruth had opened up to her and the counsellor about how she'd often been starved at home.

'The reports from her old school said that she'd often gone in without a packed lunch so they'd provided her with a school dinner and then sent the bill to her parents.

'Ruth said her stepmum had been furious about this and, as a punishment, she wasn't allowed meals at home.'

Poor Ruth had explained that she'd stopped telling the school when she didn't have any lunch with her as sometimes she'd go for days with hardly any food.

'It's not something that's going to go away overnight,' I said.

'Thanks for raising it, Maggie,' said Liz. 'I'll talk to Liberty about it and she can chat to Mum and perhaps do some work on it with Ruth.

'I'll explain how important it is for Sharon to understand Ruth's need to see, smell and taste food, about how she needs to be able to see that food is there and that it's not going to be taken away.'

'I don't think there's any quick fix,' I said. 'Just having bowls of fruit and packets of crisps around the house isn't going to solve the problem.'

I knew that it wasn't even about the food itself. This was about Ruth needing six years of love, care and warmth to be poured back into her. I'd started doing that and now Sharon needed to take over.

*

Soon it was time for Ruth to go to her mum's house for the first time and spend the night. As I drove her there she was desperately excited about seeing the house and having a sleepover. I was worried that Sharon's cottage was going to be a disappointment after all the bragging about a mansion. But as I pulled up outside the row of terraces, Ruth had a big grin on her face.

'I knew it was going to be like this,' she said. 'It's just as I imagined.'

The front door was already open and Sharon was standing there waiting.

'Come on in.' She smiled

Ruth couldn't get in the door quick enough.

'Wow,' she sighed as she walked into the living room. 'It's so big.'

She threw her arms out and started twirling around. There wasn't much room and I was worried that she'd go crashing head first into the china rabbits.

'Mind the ornaments, Ruth,' I whispered.

She couldn't wait to see the rest of the house and Sharon gave us both a tour. She'd gone to a lot of effort to make Ruth feel at home. There were framed photos of her and Ruth around the place that had been taken on their days out during contact and she'd decorated her bedroom.

Ruth was delighted with it. There was a pink duvet on the bed, furry cushions and a pink and yellow rug.

'It's lovely,' said Ruth. 'I wish I had a pink room at your house, Maggie.'

'I wanted you to feel at home and I know you like nice pretty things, like me,' Sharon told her.

I could see that Sharon was both thrilled and relieved. She

must have been nervous about Ruth coming to her house for the first time and she was keen for her to feel at home there.

Ruth seemed fine so I kept it short and sweet. I had a cup of tea and she was happy to wave me off.

'I'll leave you two to it,' I told them. 'Have a good time. Any problems, give me a ring. I'm at home tonight.'

I didn't hear anything from them, and Sharon dropped Ruth back as planned the next day.

'How did it go?' I asked Ruth when Sharon had gone.

'It was great,' she said. 'We went shopping and Mum bought me some more things for my bedroom and we went out for tea.

'It went so quickly, though,' she sighed. 'When can I go and live there for ever?'

'If you're sure that's what you want then hopefully very soon, lovey,' I told her.

The clock was ticking now. We were two months into therapy and a decision had to be made about whether Ruth was definitely going to go and live with her mum. Liz and I had a meeting with Liberty.

'How have the sessions with Ruth and Sharon been going?' Liz asked.

'Good,' said Liberty. 'It's clear that Ruth wants to go and live with her mum and we've talked about why Mum left and how Ruth felt about being left behind with her father and David.'

She explained that Ruth was incredibly loyal to her mum and didn't blame her for what had happened.

'She's not angry or resentful about her leaving them,' she said. 'In fact, she understands why Mum went because of what happened to her.

'She says her dad was horrible to her mum just like he was horrible to her.

'We can't predict what's going to happen in the future but as far as I'm concerned we've gone over it as much as we can.'

Liz agreed.

'Sharon's shown her commitment to Ruth over the past few months so I'm all for the move,' she said. 'I think it's the best possible scenario.'

I still had one main worry.

'Are you convinced that Sharon wears the trousers and not Ruth?' I asked.

'I agree with you, Maggie, that Sharon needs to remember that she's the parent and she mustn't bow to all of Ruth's demands,' said Liberty. 'However, I think that will develop over time when this initial honeymoon period has worn off. She'll find her own way.'

There was a week left before school broke up for the long summer holidays.

'Ruth could spend the first four weeks of the holidays finishing off the counselling and then move and have two weeks settling into her new home with Sharon before she starts her new school in September,' said Liz.

'That makes sense,' I said. 'It would be a lot easier for her going in on the first day of a new term along with everyone else rather than having to start later on her own.'

It would make her less of the new girl.

We all agreed this was the best plan and Liz said she'd come round and talk to Ruth that night. I pretended to be busy in the kitchen while the pair of them chatted in the front room. Ten minutes later Ruth came running in.

'Guess what, Maggie?' She grinned. 'I'm going to go and live with my mum.'

Liz followed her into the kitchen.

'Ruth and I have had a chat and she's decided that's what she wants to do,' said Liz.

Presenting it in this way meant that Ruth felt that she had some control and that she was the one making the decisions, rather than being told what was happening.

'Well, if that's what you want, then that's brilliant,' I said. 'You know we're all going to miss you dreadfully but I'm so pleased that it's worked out for you and your mum. I really am.

'You've got so much to look forward to,' I told her. 'The end of term's coming up, there's the summer holidays and then you'll be moving.'

'I know,' she said. 'I can't wait.'

At the end of term each year group at Ruth's school had an assembly at which Mr Mattison would give out certificates to certain students for their achievements. I always tried to go to the assemblies at school as it was important for kids' self-esteem and for them to know that you cared. Ruth grinned at me from the bench where she was sitting on the stage. She hadn't been chosen to do a reading or a poem but she looked pleased to see that I was there. Soon it was time for the certificates and various children were called up and given a prize for their academic achievements.

'And now the certificate for the pupil who has made the most improvement this year,' said Mr Mattison.

'I'm proud to present this to Ruth from class 7C.'

Ruth looked stunned as she went up to get her certificate.

I was so pleased for her. She deserved every bit of that award for the way that she'd turned herself around. I think her fellow pupils felt the same as I did, as they clapped and cheered when Mr Mattison presented her with her certificate.

'Well done,' I mouthed, blowing her a kiss.

A woman who I recognised as the PE teacher and netball coach came over to me afterwards.

'You must be so proud of Ruth,' she said.

'Oh, I am.' I smiled.

'She mentioned that she's leaving school and going to live with her mum. Is that right?' she asked.

'Yes,' I said. 'Yes, it is. She'll be starting a new school in September.'

'The netball team won't be the same without her,' she said. 'She's a great little player.'

I was surprised but pleased that Ruth had shared the news about her mum with other people. As I left the hall that day, I was brimming with pride for Ruth and all she had achieved. But at the same time I couldn't help but feel sad as in four short weeks we would be saying goodbye to her for good.

SEVENTEEN

Leaving

As soon as school finished, Liz, Liberty and I had another meeting to finalise all the details.

'The plan for the next four weeks is that Ruth will be having two three-night stays at Sharon's,' said Liz. 'They'll both have a therapy session with Liberty on the Friday and Sharon will drive them to her house. Then she'll bring them back on the Monday, they'll have another session and Sharon will drop Ruth back to you, Maggie.'

It sounded fine to me. The idea was to build up the time Ruth spent at her new house. She could also start taking some of her things with her.

'At the end of the four weeks Ruth will move to Sharon's permanently.

'Is everyone happy with that?'

'I think it's getting to the point where I've taken my work as far as I can with Ruth,' said Liberty. 'As she gets older she might want to have counselling again as different thoughts and feelings come up.'

I knew from other children I'd looked after who had been sexually abused that as they began their first relationships as older teenagers a whole different set of issues came up. Counselling would definitely be useful in the future.

It was agreed that Liberty would visit Ruth at her mum's and do a final session and talk everything through with both of them and then go down the following week to say goodbye.

'You look deep in thought, Maggie,' said Liz. 'What is it?'

I was thinking about the damaged, terrified child Ruth had been when she first came to me, compared to the girl I was about to say goodbye to. When I'd heard about the abuse and neglect she'd suffered I'd understood why she was like that. She'd caused so much disruption in our family at first but, over time, I had grown to love her.

'Whatever happens, Ruth's a survivor,' I said. 'She has so much strength and determination and now she knows how to use that in a positive way.

'I still worry that Sharon might not be strong enough to handle the issues that are bound to come up.'

'Well, as Ruth's social worker I'm still going to be visiting them once a week so I'll be there to support them,' said Liz.

'Right, is everyone happy?'

I nodded. I really was. I was happy for Ruth that she was finally moving on and having a fresh start with her mum.

As a foster carer, I always like to do something when a long-term placement leaves to mark the event in some way. By the time Ruth left she would have been part of our family for ten months. It's nice for the child to know that they're wanted and they will be missed and it's good for the other kids in the house to have a chance to say goodbye.

I didn't think it was right to make a huge fuss about Ruth going, however, as I didn't want to make her connection to us any stronger. I wanted her to know that we would miss her but that we were happy for her as she went to live with her mum. It was my job to help her move on and not make her feel sad that she was leaving us.

'How do you fancy having a barbecue on your last day here?' I suggested to her.

I was keen to keep it low-key so I didn't want to call it a party.

If we had a barbecue in the afternoon people could drop in as and when they wanted.

'Who would you like me to invite?' I asked.

'What about Heidi and her kids, Vicky and her lot and Marion too?' she said.

'Good idea,' I told her.

They were all the people that she'd spent time with over the past ten months.

'What about David?' I asked. 'I think it's important that you say goodbye to him.'

She hadn't seen her brother for a couple of months, ever since he'd decided that he didn't want anything to do with their mum.

'He can come if he wants, as long as he's not going to be cross with me for going to live with Mum,' she said.

'He won't be,' I told her. 'I'll make sure he's on his best behaviour.'

Liz had told me that David had moved to his new foster carer's.

She was a woman called Andrea who I vaguely knew so I gave her a call and told her what was happening.

'I wondered if David would like to come and say goodbye to Ruth?' I said. 'His mum isn't going to be there so he doesn't have to worry about that.'

I asked her if she'd mind coming with him as I didn't want him to say anything to upset Ruth or be negative or put doubts into her head about going to live with their mum.

'I think it's important for him to be there but I'd really appreciate it if you'd stay to keep an eye on him.'

Thankfully she agreed to bring him along.

As it was the summer holidays, I planned a few treats and trips out as a way to say goodbye to Ruth. One day Lily was at a friend's house and Louisa was out with her mates.

'How about you and I go shopping and get you a few bits and pieces to take to your mum's?' I said.

'Yeah, that would be great.' Ruth smiled.

I knew how much she loved shopping.

We were in Next when she saw a long, flowery sundress.

'I love this,' she said.

'Why don't you try it on?'

She looked so pretty in it, I couldn't resist buying it for her. Unlike most of the clothes she used to be drawn to, it wasn't too grown-up or revealing.

'You look lovely,' I said. 'I'd really like to get that for you. You can wear it for the barbecue and then take it to your mum's.'

I got her a headband too that was like a flowery crown.

'Thank you, Maggie,' she said.

I also planned a day out for all of us at a theme park, and Marion and her kids came along. The children absolutely loved it and tore around excitedly, deciding what ride to go on next. Louisa was desperate for us all to go on the log flume.

'No way,' said Ruth. 'I'm not going on that.'

'Go on,' said Louisa. 'Surely you're not scared of a little bit of water?'

'If I'm going on it, then you are,' I told Ruth. 'I don't think we'll get that wet.'

We sat in the same carriage and as we inched higher and higher up towards the steep drop, I wrapped my arms around her and she pressed herself into my body.

'Don't worry, I've got you,' I reassured her, although I was secretly terrified too.

I don't know who was screaming louder – me or Ruth – as we shot down into the water and got absolutely drenched. Our screams turned to hysterical laughter as we looked at each other.

'Maggie, you told me it wouldn't be that bad,' she said, water dripping down her nose.

'You look like a drowned rat,' I howled.

Thankfully, at the end of the ride the kids spotted some huge drying machines. There were shrieks of excitement as we stepped inside the booth and warm jets of air shot out of the sides to dry our clothes.

Marion and I watched the kids as they walked ahead of us, chattering and laughing. Ruth was in the thick of it, getting on with everyone.

'It's incredible when I think back to how she used to be,' said Marion. 'God, she was so stroppy.'

Marion was right. Ruth was always the one causing all the arguments, proclaiming everything wasn't fair and generally getting on everyone's nerves. She always hung on the sidelines and refused to get involved in anything and the way she was back then, the other kids didn't want her to.

On the way home we stopped at a country pub to break up the journey. It was a lovely evening so we sat outside in the beer garden and had dinner. We all chose fish and chips and they were huge portions.

'I can't eat any more,' said Ruth, pushing away her plate that was still half full. 'I've had enough.'

It was the first time I'd ever seen her leave any food on her plate or acknowledge that she felt full and it was another milestone.

The kids were all shattered and on the way home there was silence in the back of the car as it got dark and they started to nod off.

'That was the best day ever,' sighed Ruth before she closed her eyes.

As I looked at the three sleeping children in the back and enjoyed the peace, I knew Ruth was right. It didn't happen very often but today had been one of those picture-perfect days that all of us would always look back on with a smile. The sun had shone, there had been no arguments, everyone had got on and there had been lots of fun and laughter. It was the perfect memory to send Ruth off with.

The next few days were spent sorting out her possessions. Shortly before she left I went through all the craft stuff and the toy boxes, putting the things that I knew were hers to one side.

'You have a look yourself and check that I haven't missed anything,' I told her.

The kids all loved going to car boot sales and bought so many bits and bobs with their pocket money that I often lost track of what belonged to whom. Lily helped her go through the toy box.

'Remember when you thought you weren't allowed to keep your presents?' she said when Ruth came across some Lego she'd got for Christmas.

'Do you believe me now?' asked Lily.

'Yes.' Ruth laughed. 'I believe you. I know I can keep them.'

The Lego was still in the box and she hadn't even opened it.

'Do you want this, Lily?' she asked her.

Lily was so delighted, she came running over to me.

'Maggie, Maggie, Ruth has given me her Lego. Can I have it? Please say yes.'

I'd had children in the past that had given their toys or books to another child only to demand them back at a later date and cause lots of upset. So now the rule in my house was that the swapping or giving of toys had to be agreed by me before it happened.

'Ruth, are you sure you want to give your Lego away to Lily?'

She nodded.

'I've never played with it and I know she'll like it.'

The deal was done and Lily was delighted. I knew the old Ruth would have taken great delight in taunting Lily and there was no way she would have ever willingly given her anything. But over time a nice bond had developed between the pair of them and I knew they were going to miss each other.

Ruth's long weekends with Sharon had gone well and soon it was her last full day with us before Liz collected her in the morning. Before the barbecue started, Ruth came to me with her hairbrush, some bobbles and her new headband.

'Maggie, will you do my hair for me?' she asked.

I was about to say I was too busy rushing around trying to get everything ready before the guests arrived, then I looked at her pleading face. This was probably going to be the last time that I could do this for her and I knew how much it meant. This was our special time when we chatted and Ruth relaxed and opened up to me.

'OK,' I said. 'French plait or a ponytail?'

'Plait please – and my new headband.'

As I sat there plaiting her hair I could tell she was going to miss this.

'You'll have to ask your mum to do your hair,' I said to her.

'I already did but she said she's not very good at it,' she sighed. 'She told me she doesn't know how to do a French plait.'

'I'm sure she can learn,' I said, but Ruth didn't look convinced.

Soon the guests started arriving. Heidi came over with her kids, as did Marion and Vicky, so there were quite a few of us. It was a warm August day so I opened the French doors in the dining room so the kids could run in and out. I put some music on, and the sausages, burgers and chicken sizzled away on the barbecue. Ruth was enjoying being the centre of attention. Everyone had brought her cards and Heidi's children had got her a soft toy dog. She danced around the garden in her new dress, smiling and chatting to everyone and asking what they'd like to eat from the barbecue.

I was struck by how sociable she was. She asked people questions about themselves; it wasn't just all about her any more. She'd changed so much in the way she laughed, the way she hugged people and was able to have fun rather than spend her time causing battles and confrontations. She wasn't a ghost girl any longer. She was a real person who felt good enough to be loved and wanted, and could love people back in return.

Halfway through the afternoon David arrived with his foster carer Andrea. Ruth seemed pleased to see him but I could tell that she was nervous around him and there was a tension between them. I made sure I had a chat with him as I wanted him to know that I was grateful to him for coming.

'How do you feel about Ruth moving in with your mum?' I asked.

'If that's what she wants then that's fine, but I don't really know her,' he said. 'I wish all this had never happened and I was still living with my dad and Marie.'

I still found it bizarre that two children from the same family, living in the same house, could have such different experiences.

Part of me felt sad for him. Unlike Ruth, he had too much anger and blame to live with his mum so he was going to spend the rest of his childhood in the care system.

'Ruth might be leaving but I'm not going anywhere, David,' I told him. 'You've got my phone number, so if you ever need to talk, you know where I am.'

'Thanks,' he said.

After serving everyone their food, I finally had a chance to sit down. Ruth came and perched on a camping chair next to me on the grass.

'So, do you think you're going to miss us?' I asked her.

'I'll miss doing things like this,' she said, looking round at the garden full of people. 'I think it's going to be a lot quieter at my mum's.'

We sat there tucking into our burgers.

'Who will be coming to live with you next?' she asked.

I shrugged.

'I don't know, flower,' I said. 'It's a bit like when you came to me. I get a phone call and it's all very quick and I have to say yes or no.'

'Are you pleased that you said yes to me?' she asked.

'Of course I am,' I told her.

She smiled.

'Ruth, come and see this,' Lily shouted to her.

'Go on,' I said. 'You go and play.'

She got up and was about to wander off but then she stopped, turned round, ran back and gave me a big hug.

'What was that for?' I asked.

'No reason.' She grinned.

I smiled too. She was so, so different from the stroppy girl who had arrived on my doorstep ten months ago.

That night, when everyone had gone, the four of us sat in the garden.

'I've got something for you, Ruth,' Louisa said.

She handed over her collection of pens, pencils and erasers.

'Oh wow,' gasped Ruth, who was both shocked and delighted that Louisa had given her her most treasured possessions. 'Thanks so much.'

'Do you know what?' said Louisa. 'I think, in a funny way, I'm going to miss you.'

Ruth smiled. The pair of them hadn't always seen eye to eye but Louisa had grown very fond of her. It was a bit like having an annoying little sister.

I didn't believe in giving children big presents before they left, as over the months they were with me they always accumulated so much stuff. However, the day before I'd seen a dainty silver bracelet in a local gift shop and I hadn't been able to resist getting it for Ruth.

'And here's a little something to remember me by,' I said, handing her the tiny package.

'I really love it, Maggie. Thank you,' she said, putting it straight on.

Ruth was still very pleased to be going to live with her mum. I knew there was a part of her that was sad to leave us and I knew she was going to miss us, but the excitement of going to live with her mum overrode that.

That night as I was walking past her bedroom, I heard her calling to me.

'Maggie, please will you tuck me in?'

'Of course I will,' I said, smoothing down her duvet around her.

'Just think, this time tomorrow night you'll be going to sleep in your lovely new pink bedroom,' I told her. 'Are you looking forward to it?'

'Yes,' she said. 'I will miss you, though.'

'And we'll miss you but you know where we are if you need us.'

I went downstairs and did the last bit of clearing up after the barbecue. Thankfully it was all quiet upstairs until around 11 p.m. when I heard creaking on the landing. I poked my head around the living room door to find Ruth sitting on the stairs in her nightie.

'What on earth are you doing up at this time?' I asked her.

'I couldn't sleep,' she said.

'Come on then. Come down and have a hot chocolate with me in the kitchen.'

Ruth scampered down the stairs, smiling. I wouldn't normally have done that but it was her last night with us and I knew it was probably last-minute nerves keeping her awake.

We sat in the kitchen and chatted over our steaming mugs of hot chocolate. We talked about her new school and all the things she and her mum planned to do together.

'You've got so much to look forward to,' I told her.

I also talked about how much I thought she'd changed in the ten months that she'd been with us.

'When you first came to live here you were like a little fireball of rage,' I told her and she smiled. 'You were so cross and grumpy and angry at the world.

'But I understood why you were like that after everything that you'd been through and I wanted to try and help you.'

'Do you think I'm different now?' she asked.

'Of course you are,' I said. 'Look at you today at the barbecue. Going round chatting to everyone and checking what they wanted to eat. Laughing and playing with all the other kids. You know how to have fun now.'

'I was a bit of a pain when I first came, wasn't I?' she said and we both grinned.

Thankfully our chat seemed to settle Ruth and she went back to bed. When I checked on her half an hour later she was fast asleep.

In the morning Liz arrived to collect Ruth. She was taking her to therapy first then she was driving her to Sharon's house. Most of her stuff was already down there. She just had her favourite things that she'd left until last and her clothes and toiletries from the past few days.

'Have you got everything?' I asked. 'Liz is waiting outside.'

I believe it's always best for a child (and for me!) to keep goodbyes short and sweet. It's not helpful for a child to see me break down or get upset.

Ruth was clutching Kit Cat – the soft toy that I'd bought her to see her through the court case. Lily, Louisa and I went outside to wave her off. She gave them both a hug then it was my turn to say goodbye. I took a deep breath and swallowed the lump in my throat. I was determined to keep it together.

'Bye, lovey,' I said, giving her a cuddle. 'Keep in touch and remember we're always here if you need us.'

'Bye,' she said and when she looked up at me I noticed that her eyes were filled with tears.

'Don't be sad,' I told her. 'You're going to be so happy at your mum's.'

'I know,' she said. 'I'm just going to miss you.'

'And we'll miss you too,' I said, giving her another cuddle. 'Now off you go. I bet your mum will be waiting for you and you can get settled in that lovely new bedroom of yours.'

Ruth smiled and we all watched as she got into the back of Liz's car. The tears were gone and she grinned and waved at us through the glass.

'I'll ring you,' Liz mouthed to me through the window.

'Bye bye,' yelled Lily as the engine started and they pulled away. 'Enjoy your swimming pool.'

I gave her a puzzled look.

'Swimming pool?' I asked.

'Well, she was always going on about how her mum had a pool in the back garden,' she said.

I couldn't stop myself from laughing and the lump in my throat was gone.

After Ruth had left I went into the living room with Lily and Louisa. As I sat down on the settee, I felt so sad and drained. I hadn't realised how utterly exhausting the past ten months had been.

'Who's going to come and live with us now?' asked Lily.

'I don't know,' I said. 'Hopefully we'll have a few days to get over Ruth leaving first.'

It was nice to be just the three of us again, even if it was only temporary.

'I suppose you're going to start painting the bedroom tomorrow?' Louisa asked.

I laughed.

'You know me so well,' I said.

After a long-term placement had left I always liked to give the room a new lick of paint ready for whoever would be in there next. It was also a way to help me move on emotionally.

'Can we have another colour instead of that boring yellow?' she asked.

I thought back to how upset Ruth had been when I'd first decorated her room and dismantled her bed. That all seemed so long ago now.

'We'll see,' I told her. 'Maybe a change will do us all good.'

When I went upstairs later I passed Ruth's bedroom. I was too tired to even contemplate tidying up in there today. *I'll start sorting things out tomorrow*, I thought as I closed the door.

'Come on, kids, let's go out for lunch,' I called out.

I knew it was hard for Lily and Louisa too when our family unit changed. I wanted them to feel secure and settled, and to reassure them that I was always there for them. They seemed fine about Ruth leaving. I think because she was going to live with her mum they saw it as a good thing. She was going back to family, it didn't feel the same as when kids were adopted.

The three of us spent a quiet day together and when I went to sleep that night I couldn't help but think of Ruth in her pink bedroom at her mum's. I wondered how it was going and hoped that they were both happy.

EIGHTEEN

Flowers and Rainbows

The next day I woke up early, before Lily and Louisa. It was a bright, sunny morning and I crept downstairs and made myself a cup of tea. I sat at the kitchen table, enjoying the peace and thinking about Ruth waking up in her new home with her mum. I hoped that she'd had a good night's sleep.

As I still hadn't heard a peep from the other two, I decided to make a start on cleaning Ruth's room. I hadn't been in there since she left and when I walked in I was struck by how bare – and tidy – it looked without her toys and books strewn all over the floor and heaps of clothes piled everywhere. I opened the window to let some fresh air in and plugged the hoover in. I was about to start stripping the bed when I noticed something lying on top of the mattress.

I went over and picked it up. It was a beautiful painting of a row of brightly coloured flowers. I managed to hold it together until I read the message written on the bottom.

Love u Maggie. Thank u. Ruth xxoo

I sat down on the bed and hot, salty tears streamed down my

face. I didn't even notice that Louisa had come in until I saw her standing beside me.

'Are you OK?' she asked, putting her arm around me.

'Oh, I'm fine.' I smiled, quickly wiping my tears away. 'I'm just being a big old softie, that's all.'

I showed her Ruth's painting.

'Isn't it gorgeous?' I said. 'She must have done it for me at therapy.'

It was such a lovely gesture. It had really touched me.

We went downstairs to the kitchen and I pinned the painting up so it had pride of place on the noticeboard.

When Lily finally got up we had a quiet day of sorting and cleaning. Lily spent the afternoon building Lego.

'I wish Ruth was here to play with me,' she sighed. 'She was good at thinking up things to make.'

'I'll play with you,' I offered.

'No thanks,' she said. 'It's not the same.'

I could see she was missing her. I think in a way Louisa did too.

'It feels weird without her, doesn't it?' she said.

'We'll get used to it,' I told her. 'Let's try and enjoy just being the three of us again.'

Whenever a child who had been with us for several months left it took a while for us to adjust.

Living with Ruth had been an emotional rollercoaster at times, but we had all got attached to her and grown to love her. Our house was going to be very different without her around, and although I was feeling sad and tearful about it, I wanted to be positive for Louisa and Lily.

Later that morning Liz phoned.

'How are you?' she asked.

'It's all very quiet and strange,' I said. 'How did Ruth seem when you dropped her off yesterday?'

'She didn't say much in the car on the way down there,' said Liz. 'But when we got to Mum's, she seemed fine.

'Sharon was pleased to see her and she'd made her a special pink cake. I stayed for a quick cup of tea and then I left them to it.'

I was relieved to hear that it had gone well and there had been no tears or tantrums.

'I've been thinking about her all night, wondering how she's getting on,' I said.

'She'll be absolutely fine,' said Liz. 'She's a tough little cookie.

'I know we both have our concerns, Maggie, but we've got to leave them to get on with it and find their own way.

'I'll be going down to see them every week and Liberty's got a session with them next week, so Ruth's going to have lots of support and people around her to make sure she's happy.'

'I know,' I said.

Over the years I'd learnt how to physically let go and say goodbye to a child but emotionally it always took me a lot longer.

As Liz was Ruth's social worker, we wouldn't be in regular contact any more.

'I'm sure our paths will cross again,' she told me. 'But thank you for all your hard work and commitment to Ruth.

'I know it wasn't easy at times but you got her through one of the most difficult things she's ever had to face in her life.

'You did an amazing job, Maggie – she's like a different girl.'

'That was all down to Ruth,' I said. 'I just helped her along the way.'

I was enormously proud of what she'd come through and what she'd become.

'It's been hard work, Liz. I won't deny that,' I said. 'And I know it sounds corny but it really has been a privilege.'

'Well, I know Ruth will never forget you,' she said.

Over the next few days I planned lots of fun activities to try and cheer Lily and Louisa up. I wanted them to enjoy the last part of the summer holidays before school started again, so we went swimming and I took them on a day trip to the seaside.

We'd just walked through the door that evening when someone rang the doorbell. I was surprised to see Liberty, Ruth's counsellor, standing there.

'Hi, Maggie,' she said. 'I've been to see Ruth and Sharon today and I hope you don't mind but Sharon asked me if I could pop in and give you these.'

She handed me a beautiful bunch of pink roses with a card.

Thank you for everything, Maggie. Love from Sharon and Ruth xx

'That's really kind of them,' I said. 'How are they getting on?'

'It all seems to be going well,' she told me.

'Good,' I said and I was genuinely pleased.

Although I was desperate to ask her questions and find out more, I knew I wasn't allowed to. I wasn't Ruth's carer any more so Liberty wouldn't be able to discuss her with me because of confidentiality. The same applied to Liz as Ruth's social worker. That was the system and I knew I had to respect it.

'When you see them again say hello from me and send them my love,' I said.

'I will do,' said Liberty.

I hadn't made any arrangements to see Ruth after she'd gone and I'd left it completely up to her whether she stayed in touch. I would have been happy to go down and visit her if she had wanted but I knew that request had to come from Ruth. She'd never asked me if I was coming to see her and I knew Ruth was very much a girl who lived in the here and now. She boxed people up in her life and I suspected that Lily, Louisa and I would become one of her boxes that had been closed and taped over. That was her choice and I had to accept that.

When babies or younger children were adopted, I would always make plans to go and visit them after six weeks. That was important for little ones so they didn't think that I'd suddenly disappeared from their life or had abandoned them. But with older children like Ruth it was different. It wasn't like she'd been adopted by strangers either; she'd gone back to her mum, her own flesh and blood. I wasn't sure if it would be helpful to Ruth and Sharon to stay in touch with us. They both needed to let go of the past in order to move forward to their future together, and I was part of that past. If they wanted to let me go then I understood.

A few days later my supervising social worker Rachel came round to see me.

'I thought I'd pop in and check how things have been without Ruth,' she said. 'Did she get off OK?'

'She was fine,' I said. 'She was very excited about going to live with her mum.'

'And how are you?' she asked.

'To be honest, I'm enjoying the peace and having some downtime while it lasts,' I said.

I knew that Rachel would want to talk to me about whether I wanted to put my name back on Social Service's list to say that I had a vacancy. After a foster placement ended it was my choice whether to foster another child straight away or have a few days or weeks off. Usually I liked to get straight back into it and keep myself busy with a new challenge. I knew it would stop me dwelling on Ruth and help me to move on. Also, I quite enjoyed this part of the job – the feeling of the unknown. Not knowing what was round the corner, wondering who would be coming to me next, what they'd be like, what their problems were, where they'd come from, and then working out how I could help them.

'I know you'll be asking me in a minute, and I'm happy for you to put me down as having a vacancy,' I said.

'Actually, I did want to talk to you about that,' said Rachel. 'I've already got another child in mind for you.

'Liz has been in touch about David.'

'David?' I said. 'As in Ruth's brother?'

'Yep,' she said. 'He's having a hard time at the minute.'

She explained that David had only lasted a couple of weeks at his new carer's and they were now looking at moving him again.

'He's struggling to settle anywhere,' she said. 'This will be his third move and Liz wondered, as you know him and you know the family history, whether you'd consider taking him?'

It was a bit of a shock.

'I don't know what to say,' I told her.

'Have a think about it and I'll let Liz know,' she said.

Compared to Ruth, David at first had seemed like the easier child. But as Ruth had become more settled and stable, he had become more angry and harder to manage. Ruth had caused enough upheaval for Louisa and Lily. I didn't think it was fair to bring another troubled, disruptive child into the house right now, especially one as old as David, and I was worried it would lead to conflict. It would also feel a bit like I was betraying Ruth by taking in her brother, whom she hadn't really got along with.

'I don't need to think about it,' I told Rachel. 'I have a lot of sympathy for David, I really do, but I'm sorry, I can't take him.

'I don't think it would work and it wouldn't be fair on the kids I already have here.'

'Tell Liz I'm sorry that I can't help,' I told her. 'And say that David's got my number so he can ring me for a chat whenever he wants.'

'No problem,' she said. 'I understand.'

I felt guilty but I told myself not to. If David had been placed with me as soon as he came into the care system, I believe I could have made a difference. However, he'd told me himself that he wanted to go back to the same family who had starved and abused his sister. After everything that I knew Ruth had gone through I would have found it impossible to get my head around this and help him. It would also have felt disloyal to Ruth. I felt for him, I really did, but sadly I knew I had made the right decision.

Soon the new term started and Lily and Louisa went back to school. I got an email from Liz telling me that Sharon had registered Ruth at her local secondary school and she was due to start there that week.

Could you let the head at her old school know and say the new school will be in touch to get hold of her records?

A few days later I made an appointment to see Mr Mattison.

'How are things?' he asked. 'Did Ruth go and live with her mum in the end?'

'Yes, it's all fine,' I said. 'She's been there a couple of weeks and by all accounts it's going well.'

'Thank goodness for that,' he sighed. 'I thought you were coming to tell me that everything had fallen through and she needed her place back.'

'Thankfully no.' I smiled. 'She starts at her new school today.

'I just wanted to tell you that she'd gone and also to thank you for everything that you did for her.'

Mr Mattison smiled.

'It's a pleasure,' he said. 'Once we'd got rid of the silly attitude, she was a lovely girl.

'You know I'm happy to help anytime.'

'I really appreciate that,' I said.

'Have you heard from Ruth?'

I shook my head.

'No,' I said. 'And somehow I don't think I will.'

There were some children you knew that you'd always keep in touch with but that tended to be when they were little or because I'd struck up a genuine friendship with their adopters. Sharon and I had been perfectly pleasant to each other but we hadn't spent enough time together to form a friendship and, to be honest, neither of us had wanted to. I knew she wouldn't be encouraging Ruth to keep in touch with me. They wanted a fresh start and a new life together, and our family wasn't part of that. We'd only remind them both of the past and what they'd been through. Sharon didn't want to dwell on the past and think about Ruth being in care, and Ruth didn't want to think about the court case and what her dad had done to her. They both wanted to wipe the slate clean and I completely understood that. Ruth was a clever little thing and I was sure that her new school would be a fresh start for her. For once, she was just like everyone else. She'd be able to go into her new school and say: 'I live with my mum.'

As I walked back home from the school, I ended up wandering down our road at the same time as the postman. When he saw me going up the path to my front door, he followed me and handed me the post.

'Just one for you today,' he said, handing me an envelope.

Inside was a postcard with a brightly coloured rainbow on the front. The rainbow had a smiley face on it. As I turned it over to read the message, I recognised the writing straight away.

All it said was:

Bye bye, Maggie.

The rest of the space was filled with kisses.

Although it didn't have her name on it, I knew it was from Ruth. It was her way of saying goodbye and I knew in my heart that that would be the last time I'd ever hear from her.

I was pleased that at least we'd had a goodbye. Ruth had never had the chance to say goodbye to her dad or Marie, the woman she believed was her mum, or her half-brothers. Saying goodbye is important because it gives children an ending. It allows them to draw a line under the past so they can move on.

That was my one big hope for Ruth – that she was finally able to let go of her past and move forward to the future. I hoped that she was able to say goodbye to all the hurt, pain and fear that had ruled her life for so long. With her dad safely behind bars, I wanted her to enjoy her new life with her mum. To love and be loved, to feel wanted and secure so that ghost of a girl never, ever came back.

Acknowledgements

Thank you to my children, Tess, Pete and Sam, who are such a big part of my fostering today even though I had not met you when Ruth came into my home. To my wide circle of fostering friends – you know who you are! Your support and your laughter are valued. To my friend Janette and her boys, Andrew B for your continued encouragement and care, and to Heather Bishop who spent many hours listening and enabled this story to be told. Thanks also to my agent Rowan Lawton and to Anna Valentine at Orion for giving me the opportunity to share these stories.

To contact

Maggie Hartley:

EMAIL

maggie.hartley@orionbooks.co.uk

OR GO TO

facebook.com/maggiehartleyauthor

Also by

MAGGIE HARTLEY

Out now in eBook and paperback

Out now in eBook

TRAPEZE

COMING SOON

Out in eBook
December 2016

Out in eBook
April 2017

Out in paperback
June 2017

Out in eBook
July 2017

Out in paperback
September 2017